FINALLY, FAMILY DEVOTIONS THAT WORK

FINALLY

FAMILY DEVOTIONS
THAT WORK

TERRY HALL

MOODY PRESS
CHICAGO

To
Herb and Judy Koonce
and their children,
Heather, Shawn, and Todd—
a family I deeply appreciate

© 1986 by
THE MOODY BIBLE INSTITUTE
OF CHICAGO

Library of Congress Cataloging in Publication Data

Hall, Terry, 1941–
  Finally, family devotions that work.

  1. Family—Prayer-books and devotions—English.
I. Title.   II. Title: Family devotions that work.
BV255.H32   1986   249   86-5105
ISBN 0-8024-2538-0 (pbk.)

1 2 3 4 5 6 7 Printing/LC/Year 91 90 89 88 87 86

Printed in the United States of America

CONTENTS

JANUARY

Extra! Extra! Read All About It!

Having trouble finding time for family devotions? You're not alone. It's difficult to get the whole clan together in one place, at one time, with a relaxed attitude.

And some of us don't know how to start a family worship time. One mother, convicted by a sermon, went to a religious bookstore and asked for a family altar in Early American to match her furniture.

Schedule a time and place to meet each week. Ask God for wisdom in applying these suggestions to your family's interests. Start small, and be brief. It's better to leave children and teens wanting more than to force them to sit through a dull routine.

Week One / All That's Fit to Print

Pretend you're a newspaper editor during Old Testament days. You're to produce something that looks like a modern paper, but everything in it will be based on biblical accounts.

Select a passage you are currently studying at church or choose a short Bible book such as Jonah. Read it together, preferably in a version suited to your children's learning level. Let each family member choose a different part of the paper from these options:

- headline and lead news story
- masthead
- other news columns
- "photos" (drawings, doodles, stick figures)
- want ads
- advertisements
- personalities in the news
- women's page (fashions, domestics, recipes)
- crossword puzzles
- poetry
- interviews
- maps
- small filler items
- editorials
- letters to the editor
- cartoons
- men's page (sports, travel, business)

You'll need paper, pencils, and crayons for each person. As editor, you'll gather and organize the contributions. If you want to publish your creation, photocopy machines make great printing presses.

Perhaps you don't feel creative enough to handle such a project. Consider these examples from Jonah and the sample newspaper on page 3.

- Insert an employee ad: "Prophet wanted. Must be willing to follow orders. Position requires transfer to Nineveh."
- Include a letter to the editor from the Mariners' Union decrying the lax port security allowing runaway prophets to use cargo ships.
- A "Nineveh Notes" column includes these tidbits: "Authorities Institute Religious Services in Palace Ballroom"; "Governor Returns 5 Million Stolen Rubles to Province Coffers."

THE JOPPA JOURNAL

NEWS
EDITORIALS
WEATHER
GAMES
ADVERTISEMENTS
WANT ADS

BUSINESS NEWS:
SHIPPING STOCK PLUMMETS WITH NEWS OF ENTIRE CARGO LOST AT SEA.

EXCLUSIVE:
INTERVIEW WITH GREAT FISH

"What is it like to harbor a disobedient prophet?"

"How would you describe your creator?"

EDITORIAL

At first I felt Nineveh deserved to be destroyed. But God has shown me my mistake, and now I rejoice because of their repentance.

NINEVEH NOTES

Leaders begin worship services in palace ballroom.

- Someone could write an editorial urging Jews not to hold grievances against Ninevites since God has forgiven them.
- The business page might run this headline: "Shipping Stock Plummets with News of Entire Cargo Lost at Sea."
- On the women's page, try some ads for the new fall fashions from Nineveh like "Sackcloth for a Simpler Life-style."
- If you can doodle or draw even a little, make a Joppa Travel Agency display ad for excursion tours of Tarshish: "Special economy fare at bottom prices—if you don't mind sleeping in the cargo hold."
- Print an obituary of a lesser-known person, such as Jonah's father, Amittai, or the king of Nineveh.

Interview the captain of the ship. You're not limited to people, either. Ask the fish questions: "How did you know when and where Jonah would be thrown overboard? How do you feel harboring a disobedient prophet? Did you have severe indigestion? How would you describe your Creator? What is it like to always be obedient to God?"

Discuss with your family how your news source, the Bible, differs from modern media. Read 2 Timothy 3:16–17 and ask: "What does the Bible claim for itself? What is the Bible designed to do in our lives? How would our family life be different this week if we *really* believed these two verses? In sentence prayers, thank God for the Bible and for each other.

Week Two / Memory Music

Do you ever write songs? Relax—you don't have to know music composition to use this method. This week's suggestion is graded by age, but your children's abilities should determine the projects they take on.

To age seven: Memorizing Scripture is easy for this age group, especially if set to simple, catchy melodies.

New words can be added to familiar tunes children have learned. Visit a Christian bookstore and help your child select a tape or record of Scripture set to music (such as "Sing a Song of Scripture," "Kids' Praise," or "Critter Country"). Most stores have demonstration albums to preview before you buy.

Ages eight to twelve: This age group can make up words to existing tunes, substituting one syllable per note. Sing a simple chorus or hymn, counting on your fingers the syllables in each line.

"Jesus Loves Me," for instance, has seven syllables in each of its four lines, not including the chorus. Now make up new sentences with the same number of syllables. Here's an example using Jonah. Each line summarizes one chapter of the book.

> Jonah went against God's wish;
> So he wound up in a fish!
> Nineveh turned to the Lord;
> But the worm got that old gourd!
>
> (*chorus*)
> Don't be like Jonah!
> Don't be like Jonah!
> Don't be like Jonah!
> Accept God's perfect will.

Teenagers: If your teen has some musical ability, he'll enjoy creating songs from Scripture, especially those suited for guitar accompaniment. He could also make up more sophisticated words to an existing hymn.

Referring to a hymnal tune, put one new syllable under each note of the hymn. You can always stretch a syllable over several notes, but don't "bunch" two or more syllables under one note.

You may also want to write the original words and put corresponding new words under them. Each child can work on separate lines, stanzas, or even the chorus. Or try grouping teens in pairs so they can work together.

Here's how Jonah chapter 1 might look, using the tune "What a Friend We Have in Jesus":

> God did call his prophet Jonah
> To a great and vile city
> Jonah ran away to Tarshish,
> But the Lord did stir the sea!
> Lots were cast to find the sinner,
> And the men did fear the Lord.
> They then threw the prophet over,
> But a fish took him aboard!

Even non-musical people can write poetic rhyming verse with a regular rhythm. Sing your new song a few times, and you'll be amazed at how quickly you memorize the words and concepts.

Next, read Psalm 96 together. For two minutes, list from this psalm reasons to sing God's praise. Then prayerfully do so.

Week Three / Anyone for a Game?

An easy way to enjoy learning Bible concepts or verses is to convert a "secular" game into a "scriptural" one. Many common games, such as Parcheesi, Monopoly, or Scrabble, only need to have homemade Bible questions added. Before any player takes a move, he has to answer a question card.

The following hints may help you in designing scriptural games:

1. The whole family should read a Bible portion together first and discuss its meaning.
2. Choose questions from a passage suitable to your family's age levels. It's best to have about twenty new questions each time you play.
3. Put Bible references on question cards instead of answers. When a player misses, he must look up the answer and read it aloud. He still loses his turn. But because that card is shuffled back into the playing pile, there's motivation to remember the answer.

4. Interesting twists can be added. Try including extra statements on question cards: "Correct answer gives you three extra places," or "Wrong answer sends one of your pieces back to home base."

To create a game for younger children, paste a Bible story picture from a magazine or Sunday school paper onto stiff cardboard. Cut the picture into big pieces with gently curved lines to make a simple puzzle. Hide these pieces around the house as a basis for a treasure hunt.

Members of the family can call out "warmer" as the child approaches a hidden piece. Once pieces are found and assembled, explain the story of the picture. This makes a great review of Sunday school lessons. Thank God for the privilege of being a family and enjoying His Word together.

Week Four / Guess What?

Reading Scripture can be more interesting if you ask each other questions relating to Bible facts and application. Here are some examples from Proverbs (answers are at end of chapter):

1. Why is it wrong to be completely open-minded?
2. What kind of a fool is hopeless and should be avoided?
3. How can you recognize a slothful man? What does "slothful" mean?
4. What can cause family fights?
5. What can a person do to avoid ever being kidnapped?
6. Why is it foolish to get involved in get-rich-quick schemes?
7. How do others judge you by your friends?
8. Why should we never co-sign for someone else's loan? What does "co-sign" mean?
9. What is the easiest way to break up a close friendship?
10. How can you be sure to win every argument?
11. How can a fool pretend to be wise and get away with it?

12. What could a person do to make others be attracted to him?
13. How could you conquer a person who's physically stronger than you?
14. Why should we never rejoice when our enemy falls?
15. What is the only thing worse than being a fool?
16. What is a certain shortcut to failure in life?

Of course, you can add humor in designing questions. Try these examples (answers are at end of chapter):

1. Who is the shortest man in the Bible?
2. Who is the smallest man?
3. Who is the straightest man?
4. When was tennis played in Bible times?
5. What time of day was Adam created?
6. What did Adam and Eve do after God expelled them from Eden?
7. When was a rooster's crow heard by every living creature on earth?
8. Who was the most successful physician in the Bible?
9. Who is the first Irishman mentioned in Scripture?

Questions could also be taken from a sermon or Bible study the whole family heard recently. Ask questions about missionaries you know, too, taken from one of their prayer letters.

And always ask: "What would God want me to do this week with what I have learned?" Be sure to thank Him for insights and ask His help in application.

Answers to Proverbs questions:

1. 4:20–27; 13:13–20; 14:6–8, 15; 15:14; 19:27
2. 19:19; 20:19
3. 6:6–11; 18:9; 20:4; 24:30–34; 26:13–16
4. 26:20–21
5. 13:8
6. 20:21; 23:4–5; 28:20–22
7. 13:20; 17:4; 22:24–25
8. 17:18; 22:26–27
9. 16:28; 17:9
10. 15:18; 17:14
11. 17:27–28
12. 16:7; 19:4; 27:9–10
13. 16:32
14. 24:17–18
15. 26:12; 29:20
16. 5:20–23; 6:32; 28:13; 29:1

Answers to humorous questions:

1. Knee-high-miah (Nehemiah) or Bildad the Shoe-height (Shuhite, Job 2:11)
2. Peter, the disciple who slept on his watch (Matthew 6:40)
3. Joseph, because Pharaoh made him into a ruler (Genesis 41:42–43)
4. When Joseph served in Pharaoh's court (implied in Genesis 41:38–46)
5. A little before Eve (Genesis 2:7, 21–22)
6. They raised Cain (Genesis 3:23; 4:1)
7. In Noah's ark (Genesis 7:13–23)
8. Job, because he had the most patients (patience, James 5:11)
9. Nick O'Demus (Nicodemus, John 3:1–5)

FEBRUARY

Don't Call Me Irresponsible

Family harmony depends on each member assuming personal responsibility to contribute. In God's perfect design for families, new members are born completely dependent on parents. As children develop, however, parents begin to require them to share in family responsibility.

Children need to learn early that life is not a "give-me" proposition. That might also mean cultivating a thankful spirit. Increasing age should bring increasing responsibility for personal care and accountability for one's actions.

Prayerfully plan how best to use the following Bible study material. If an idea is too lengthy for one evening, use parts of it during mealtimes and bedtimes to accomplish the lesson over several days. Family trips in the car provide other opportunities to implement selected activities.

Week One / Divided Duties

"Why do I always get blamed for everything?" "I did the dishes last night. It's Janet's turn tonight."

Sound familiar? Maintaining a list of family duties

often prevents such clashes. If you don't already have one, let the family come up with a list of regular responsibilities for each member. You can appoint a family secretary, preferably an older child, to record everybody's suggestions.

Set a two-minute time limit or a maximum of six items per list. Don't try to make the lists exhaustive, and avoid quibbling over who will do what. Use this time to build appreciation for each member's contribution to the family. If the lists are primarily activity-oriented, discuss what attitudes should be added.

God has His own lists of duties, for Himself and for us, recorded in the Bible. Probably the most famous Old Testament list is the Ten Commandments. One New Testament passage with divine duties for families is Colossians 3:12–21.

As you read this together, stop when someone spots a command. Then add it to the responsibilities list you began earlier. Some will apply only to wives, husbands, children, mothers, or fathers; others should be added to everybody's list.

Have individual family members research meanings and applications for key words such as *subjection, love,* and *obedience.* Use a dictionary or whatever Bible study helps you have. You may wish to save reports and discussion for another day.

Charades is also excellent for reinforcing biblical concepts. Select several positive qualities or attitudes you'd like to see developed in your family. Next, record them on separate slips of paper and let each member select one. Try pairing up younger children with older ones to act out their choices silently for the rest of the group to guess.

Read the Colossians verses again and discuss what attitudes we should have as we complete our daily chores. Which commanded attitude—being kind, gentle, patient, forgiving one another, or thankful—would make the most difference in your home this week?

Agree to hold one another accountable for this attitude during the next seven days. Establish reminders and

11

rewards, such as a wink when the chosen attitude is missing or verbal praise when it is exhibited.

Now offer sentence prayers of praise for each other by name. Every person should ask God to help him or her do his duties with the right attitudes.

Week Two / Simple Steps

Sometimes our prayers can't be answered until we respond in faith and obedience to God. For example, if we ask the Lord to make us better Christians, we may first have to pray regularly and read our Bibles to discover how He wants us to behave.

Make a quiz game from the following Bible questions, according to your time constraints and your family's Bible knowledge. Form two teams, even if there are only one or two persons per team, and alternate questions.

Each team may discuss an answer before announcing it to the quizmaster. Let the youngest team member, as captain, have this privilege. Allow one minute for each answer. If one team misses or gets stumped, give the other team a chance. Encourage your children to look up appropriate references in their Bibles. You can give little ones clues by miming the answers. Don't forget to provide a special dessert or treat for the winners.

1. Before God could declare Abel a righteous man, what did Abel have to do? (Bring God a blood sacrifice, Genesis 4:4; Hebrews 11:4.)
2. Trick question: How long did Cain hate his brother? (As long as he was Abel.)
3. What did Enoch like to do before God took him to heaven? (Walk with God, Genesis 5:24).
4. Before God could save eight people from a world-wide flood, what did Noah have to do? (Build an ark and enter it, Genesis 6:14, 17–18).
5. What did Moses have to do before God parted the Red Sea? (Hold his hand over the water, Exodus 14:21–22, 27.)

13

6. Before Moses received the Ten Commandments from God, what did he have to do? (Go up onto Mount Sinai, Exodus 19:2–3.)
7. Trick question: Who broke all Ten Commandments in one act? (Moses, when he threw down the two tablets of stone, Exodus 32:15–19.)
8. Before God saved Rahab and her house, what did she have to do? (Help the Jewish spies and hang a scarlet cord in her window, Joshua 2:1, 12, 17–18.)
9. Before God parted the Jordan River for Joshua and the Israelites, what did the priests have to do? (Step onto the water, Joshua 3:13.)
10. What did the children of Israel have to do before God knocked down the walls of Jericho? (Walk around them for seven days and shout after the priests blew their trumpets, Joshua 6:2–5.)

Work together to identify the preceding ten events in the picture collage on page 13.

Successful Christian living requires our cooperation. God often waits to do His part until we have done ours.

As a group, brainstorm to list responsibilities for personal spiritual growth. For example, we need to confess our sins, present our bodies as living sacrifices, worship God, read the Bible, pray, obey authorities, and share our faith.

Using a Bible concordance, older children can locate passages supporting each listed item. Have one or two read aloud the next time your family meets. Then instruct each person to decide which steps of faith he will practice daily during the following week. At the end of every day, he should evaluate in writing how well he has accomplished his goals. Ask God's help, and thank Him for doing His part.

Week Three / Sorting Out

One meaningful way to meditate on Scripture is to sort out God's responsibilities and our responsibilities.

Begin this week's session by drawing two vertical lines on a sheet of paper, dividing it into three columns. Title the left column "My Responsibility" and the right "God's Responsibility." The middle column will be labeled "Results."

Choose one or more of the verses below, and fill in your chart. Not every verse will contain information for all three columns. Have each family member individually think through the verses, one verse a day, and then meet together to discuss your conclusions.

You might want to analyze other familiar passages (John 1:12; Acts 16:31; Romans 12:1–2; 1 Corinthians 10:13; Galatians 6:2, 7–10; Ephesians 6:1–4, 11; Philippians 4:6–9).

My Responsibility	Results	God's Responsibility
John 3:16 To believe in God's Son	1. I won't perish 2. I'll have eternal life.	1. To love the world 2. To give His only Son
1 Peter 2:2 To long for the pure milk of the Word like a newborn baby	I'll grow in respect to salvation	
Psalm 1:2–3 1 To delight in the law of the Lord 2. To meditate on His law day and night	1. I'll be like a tree firmly planted by streams of water 2. I'll yield fruit in season 3. My leaf won't wither 4. I'll prosper in whatever I do	

Younger children can draw or select pictures to illustrate these verses. For example, a baby with a bottle would be appropriate for 1 Peter 2:2 or a tree by a river for Psalm 1:2–3. Teenagers can look up definitions for key words in an English or Bible dictionary.

Select one responsibility from the above list, such as delighting in God's Word, and discuss specifically how to do it this week.

Now use this chart for conversational prayer. Ask God to help each family member carry out specific responsibilities. And don't forget to thank Him for the results and for fulfilling His responsibilities.

Week Four / Letters to God

Why do people anxiously await the mailman? Because we all love to get mail. Read to your family a recent letter from a close friend or relative. Thank God for the author and pray for any needs he or she might have.

The Bible is a personal letter from God to us. He sent it to tell us everything He wants us to know about Himself, His plans, and the men, women, and children He loves. If someone so important has written such a loving and thoughtful letter as the Bible, don't you think we ought to write back?

Distribute stationery and pens for each family member to compose a letter to God. Divide the letter into three paragraphs, beginning with:

- Thank You, Lord
- Help me, Lord
- I confess, Lord

Everyone likes to receive thank-you notes. God is no exception. Start your letter by thanking the Lord for what you have learned from the Bible about Him, yourself, and your relationship. If necessary, take a moment to "prime the pump" by brainstorming a list of God's characteristics. Then thank the Lord for what He has done for you, is doing this week, and has promised to do.

Ask Him to help you with your responsibilities. The Christian life is not simply doing what comes naturally, but what comes supernaturally. None of us can handle this life apart from God's help. His power and resources are available by asking.

Next, confess to the Lord anything standing between you and Him. To confess means to agree with what God says. You can ask Him for forgiveness just as you would a friend whom you have wronged.

Now send your letter to God by reading it to Him as a personal prayer. Keep this and future letters so you can look back and see how God answers you.

Those too young to write can draw things for which they are thankful: family members, Jesus, their church, toys, pets, friends, themselves, teachers, neighbors.

Such a letter can be a personal response to a scriptural passage. Here's what one teenager wrote after reading and meditating on Psalm 119:1–16:

> Dear God,
> Thank You for sending Psalm 119 to me. Whoever wrote this psalm knew how important Your Word is, but I don't think I'm quite as convinced as he is. If I were, I would study my Bible a whole lot more than I do. Father, show me how special Your Word is and how I can integrate it into every area of my life.
>
> Thank you that there are rewards for following You by Your Word. It gives me more incentive to do what is right.
>
> The author of this psalm really enjoyed himself. He delighted in You and Your Book. He must have spent a lot of leisure time with it. I usually don't enjoy what I have to do, but I do like free-time activities. I'd be a different person if I spent more time with You and Your Word.
>
> I'm sorry when I dread having my devotions. If only I could get excited about them. Father, I know it's really a privilege and not a duty, but sometimes it's hard to feel right.

17

Help me to see things consistently from Your perspective.

> *With all my love,*
> *Bryan*

Try writing your own response letter to Philippians 4:1–13. Those who don't like to write letters can copy a Bible prayer, personalizing it as their own. For example, Philippians 1:9–11 might begin:

> *Dear God,*
> *   And this I pray, that my love may abound still more and more in real knowledge and all discernment, so that I may approve the things that are excellent . . ."*

Other adaptable Bible prayers are found in Ephesians 1:18–23, Colossians 1:3–18, and Ephesians 3:14–21. Another time, use these prayers as petitions for someone else by inserting his or her name in place of personal pronouns.

18

MARCH

Can You Summarize Last Week's Sermon?

If a Christian regularly attends Sunday morning worship services, Sunday school, Sunday evening services, and midweek Bible studies, he hears two hundred sermons and lessons a year. That's a lot of listening. But how much do we get out of it?

Some people claim church doesn't make any difference in their lives from week to week, so they no longer attend. But a teenager doesn't stop eating because he isn't physically mature in a month or a year.

Just as we decide to come home regularly for food, rest, and companionship, we must also decide to regularly attend services where God's Word is taught. It's a habit we have to develop. We can't skip church without stunting our growth as Christians. And becoming a better listener will increase our Word power.

Week One / Why Get Together?

Discuss the following questions this week, perhaps during mealtimes. Read aloud any suggested Bible passages.

1. Why is regular churchgoing important? (For worship, instruction, fellowship, service, and encouraging others.)
2. What benefits do Romans 10:17 and Revelation 1:3 promise for anyone hearing the Bible read and taught? (Faith and a special blessing.)
3. What does Hebrews 10:25 warn us not to forsake? (Regularly assembling with other believers.)
4. What does this verse say we should do when we get closer with other Christians? (Give encouragement.)
5. Where does the sentence that ends in Hebrews 10:25 begin? (v. 23, NASB*)
6. What else does Hebrews 10:24 command? (Consider how to stimulate others to love and good deeds.)
7. What does it mean to encourage someone? (To inspire with hope, to help, to spur on.)

Think of someone in your church fellowship you could encourage as a family. Consider anyone who is ill, out of work, alone, bereaved, having family problems, or elderly and unable to do heavy household chores.

Now plan how to encourage that person or family in a special way this week. Here are some suggestions: visit or call them, bring them a hot meal, baby-sit their children for an evening, or offer to help with chores as a family some Saturday morning.

One person we often forget about during the week is our pastor. Discuss how you might encourage him. Make a point of praying for him daily. This Sunday, arrive at church early, and look for newcomers to welcome. Sit near the front of the sanctuary, and smile at the pastor occasionally. Follow along in your Bible, taking notes while your pastor speaks. Later, thank him specifically for something he said or did. You might also ask him what you could do to help him during the week.

As a fun project, make a large homemade card for your pastor or Sunday school teacher. Each family member could contribute a drawing, clipping, or personal note of

*New American Standard Bible.

appreciation. When you've finished, have a conversational prayer time of thanksgiving for your church. Include any people you know well, the pastor, and several church programs. Intercession is one of the best helps for someone in need.

Week Two / What Did He Say?

What was the sermon about last Sunday? Can you remember the title or any of the pastor's main points? Ask your family these same questions.

Communication breakdown is one reason we don't retain more from sermons and Bible lessons. The five hundred most commonly used English words have more than fourteen thousand different meanings. And our minds often wander; we can think five to seven times faster than a preacher can talk.

How can we get more from sermons and lessons? Set a timer and brainstorm for three minutes. Appoint someone to record your list. It might look something like this:

- *Get enough rest Saturday night.*
- *Get up early Sunday for an unhurried breakfast.*
- *Be in harmony as a family and with other believers.*
- *Pray for the service and individual responses.*
- *Plan to worship God and encourage others.*
- *Look up Bible references as they are given.*
- *Jot down any questions that come to mind.*

Choose one or two items to implement as a family next Sunday. In addition, plan to take sermon notes. Discuss the benefits of doing this. (It makes us more active listeners, keeps our minds from wandering, enables us to recognize the sermon's organization, and aids retention.)

Notes may be short and simple. Jotting down just the highlights will double your intake.

Begin with a blank sheet of paper and a firm writing surface like a notebook or clipboard. Record the title of the message, Scripture text, speaker's name, the date, all main points, summary ideas, and any related Bible passages. Then note some personal application—"What can I do about what I've heard?"

When you come together again as a family, compare notes. Try to summarize the speaker's "big idea" in one sentence. Briefly talk through the message from your notes, giving each person opportunity to share.

Older youth could prepare a four-minute summary statement from their message notes. They should devote one minute to each of these categories:

- Explanation of the Bible text or topic
- Illustrations (stories or examples used)
- Points the pastor wanted to emphasize
- Application to our lives

Let children who couldn't take notes draw a picture representing something they learned from the service.

Check to see whether your church has a lending library of sermons on cassette tapes. If so, listen again to Sunday's message later in the week. You can give younger children practice in note taking by selecting a small portion to review.

You may also want to borrow supplementary materials such as dramatized Bible stories or Scripture set to music. Consider listening to such productions during your next extended drive as a family.

Repeating a message we've heard on Sunday increases our Wednesday retention from 20 to 70 percent. But putting a message into practice is best. We remember approximately 90 percent of what we do. Thank God for the worship service, and pray for continued fruit from the implanted Word in your lives.

Week Three / Getting Organized

One effective way to keep track of sermon notes is in a personal notebook. Spend an evening with the family making a "spiritual growth notebook" for each member, even the youngest.

Although the size of the notebook is immaterial, many prefer one about the size of a church bulletin.

Whatever you choose, get a durable vinyl or leather binder. I recommend a loose-leaf notebook with at least five sections marked by reinforced tab dividers. Label them: Sermon Notes, Personal Bible Study, Sunday School Lessons, Prayer Requests, and Miscellaneous.

Under *Prayer Requests*, record specific dates petitions were made. Allow space for when and how God answers. Such a list will build your faith by reminding you that God is working on your behalf. Try keeping a family prayer diary as well as personal ones.

Any handouts, current church bulletins, quotations, illustrations, or notes on other reading should be filed under the *Miscellaneous* section. You might also want to include dividers for goals, things to do, a personal schedule, phone numbers, and so on.

In younger children's notebooks, insert Sunday school take-home papers each week. Retell the stories illustrated by pictures often enough that each child can easily recall the Bible story for every notebook insert.

Within notebook sections, arrange topical headings alphabetically. If you put Bible references for sermon notes in the upper right-hand corner, you can file these according to Bible order, making notes from each book of the Bible easy to retrieve.

Schedule an after-dinner project for each family member to personalize his or her binder. You can decorate divider pages with cut-out pictures, calligraphy, doodles, or whatever. Be sure to print name, address, and phone number on the front or first divider page of every notebook in case it gets lost.

During the next seven days, have everyone collect spiritual insights. The one with the most at the end of the week gets to choose what to have for dinner some evening. Plan a time to share gleanings from each other's notebooks. Thank God for helping you to grow spiritually.

Call the church office to find out the Bible passage for next Sunday's sermon. Studying the same passage at home is excellent preparation for getting more from a message.

Begin by reading the passage. Agree together on a summary caption of about four words. Let's use Philippians 4:4–9 as an example. I titled Philippians 4 "Rejoice, Pray, and Think Right."

Now read the Scripture portion again, and make notes on a sheet of paper you have labeled *SPECS* (an acrostic explaining five things to look for in a Bible passage):

- *Sins* are attitudes or actions that displease the Lord and should be forsaken. None are directly stated in Philippians 4:4–9. (Some categories don't apply to every Bible chapter.)
- *Promises* are assurances or benefits from God to be claimed, but there are often conditions attached. The Lord is near (v. 5). God's peace surpasses all comprehension and will guard our hearts and minds in Christ Jesus (v. 7), but we must avoid being anxious by praying (v. 6). The God of peace will be with us (v. 9), but we have to practice Paul's commands in this portion of Scripture.
- *Examples* are good attitudes or actions to imitate. Bad ones would be listed as sins or stumbling blocks. Have a positive outlook like Paul's in Philippians 4:4–9.
- *Commands* are directions from God to obey. Rejoice in the Lord always (v. 4). Let your forbearing spirit be evident (v. 5). Let your requests be made known to God (v. 6). Think on things that are true, honorable, and so on (v. 8). Practice what we have learned from Paul (v. 9).
- *Stumbling blocks* are things God warns us to avoid. Don't be anxious (v. 6).

What should you do first? Pick one specific action from this passage to put into practice for the week. We can't do everything, but we can do something. Thank God for the life-changing power of His Word.

APRIL

Bearing the Sword by Heart

The average person utters about eighteen thousand words a day, the equivalent of a fifty-page book. In one year, most people say enough to fill sixty-six books, each about eight hundred pages long.

Would you like your speech and thoughts to be more pleasing to God as well as yourself? Tongues are like buckets, and minds are like wells—the tongue simply draws out and reveals what's stored in the mind (Luke 6:43–45).

Psalm 119:9–11 reminds us that God's Word is the only effective mind cleanser. Read Romans 12:1–2, Ephesians 5:25–27, and Hebrews 4:12.

Like many things in life, memorizing Scripture is easier when working with someone else. The process will become more enjoyable as you follow this month's suggestions.

Week One / How "Simon Says" Can Help

Begin by reading Deuteronomy 6:6, Joshua 1:8, Proverbs 7:1–3, and Colossians 3:16. What does God command us to do in these verses? (Memorize and meditate on Scripture.)

Now write the following benefits of Bible memorization on separate slips of paper. Secretly divide them among your family members. Playing charades, each person will act out one or two. Remember, only yes or no questions may be asked. If your family cannot guess within five minutes, have someone look up and read aloud the appropriate Scripture.

- Success in all we do (Joshua 1:8)
- Victory over sin (Psalm 119:9–11)
- Help in prayer (John 15:7)
- Spiritual growth (Psalm 1:2–3)
- Wisdom and skill in living (Psalm 119:97–100)
- Inner joy (Jeremiah 15:16)
- Answers for others' questions (1 Peter 3:15)
- Mental transformation (Romans 12:1–2)

One another evening, try this variation of "Simon Says." Using a Bible translation that your children can understand, choose one of the above verses or passages you would like your family to memorize. Then teach the following signals.

Begin by reciting a phrase of the verse, making a "come here" gesture with your hand. This indicates that family members should repeat in unison what you said.

Next, you ask a question about the Scripture portion without motioning with your hands. Your family must now answer your questions from the text.

Finally, hold both hands out as though you were indicating the length of something. This means they should recite the verse from the beginning as far as you have gone.

Now proceed in a rapid-fire manner with a random barrage of the signals, being careful not to push your children beyond their own levels of achievement. But don't make it too easy, or they'll lose interest. Of course, your biggest challenge might be keeping the signals straight yourself!

To demonstrate, we'll use Zephaniah 3:17. "The Lord your God is with you, He is mighty to save. He will take great delight in you, He will quiet you with His love, He will rejoice over you with singing" (NIV*).

For younger children, use just a portion of the verse. You could finish learning it on subsequent days or weeks. Here is how a dialogue might sound.

Parent: Zephaniah 3:17 ("come here" motion).
Children: Zephaniah 3:17.
Parent: What verse are we learning?
Children: Zephaniah 3:17.
Parent: "The Lord your God" ("come here" motion).
Children: "The Lord your God."
Parent: By what two names is He called?
Children: Lord and God.
Parent: "Is with you" ("come here" motion).
Children: "Is with you."
Parent: Who is with you?
Children: "The Lord your God."
Parent: ("length" motion)
Children: "The Lord your God is with you."

Once you've mastered this technique, work in pairs, teaming a younger and older child, to see who can learn the rest of the verse first. Only the older child should look at the words while he or she pumps the passage into the younger one. Then review the entire verse as a family.

To memorize the reference, recite book, chapter, and verse before and after the text. It also helps if you can associate it to something familiar.

For example, recite John 3:16. The next verse is 3:17, but let's recite Zephaniah 3:17 instead. Compare these two passages to strengthen the association. Although written seven hundred years apart, they both emphasize God's love for people.

Have each child write on an index card the verse you are memorizing as a family; put the Scripture portion on one side and its reference on the other. Encourage him to carry the card during the week to practice while waiting,

*New International Version.

walking, or doing other routine activities. Tape a copy of the verse to the bathroom mirror or some other place where it can be seen regularly. Ask the Lord to help family members obey His command to hide His word in their hearts.

Week Two / Sing It In

Read together this prayer by Isaac Watts. Then try singing it to the tune of "Amazing Grace," "O for a Thousand Tongues to Sing," "Joy to the World," or "O God Our Help in Ages Past."

> How shall the young secure their hearts,
> And guard their lives from sin?
> Thy Word the choicest rules imparts
> To keep the conscience clean.
>
> O how I love Thy holy law!
> 'Tis daily my delight:
> And thence my meditations draw
> Divine advice by night.
>
> To meditate Thy precepts, Lord,
> Shall be my sweet employ;
> My soul shall ne'er forget Thy Word.
> Thy Word is all my joy.

Now recite last week's memory verse several times, emphasizing a different word each time. For example, "*The* Lord your God is with you, He is mighty to save." "The *Lord* your God is with you, He is mighty to save." "The Lord *your* God is with you, He is mighty to save." "The Lord your *God* is with you, He is mighty to save."

Consult a Bible dictionary for help in understanding people, places, and perplexing terms. A regular English dictionary will also help explain unfamiliar words.

An exhaustive concordance, like Strong's or Young's, defines every word in the Bible from its original language. You may also want to get a reliable Bible commentary to understand words and phrases in their context. (For help in using Bible study tools, consult chapters 7 and 8 of *Off the Shelf and in Yourself*, published by Victor Books.)

Let's return to our example in Zephaniah. Look up information about the book and its author in a Bible dictionary. Then read the Book of Zephaniah—it's only three chapters long.

Summarize some ways the historical setting helps us understand the verse we are learning. As a group, answer these questions:

1. To whom was this book written? (Jews from Judah, the southern Hebrew kingdom. Israel had already been conquered and scattered by Assyria.)
2. What bad news did the author have to deliver? (His readers were about to be conquered by the Babylonians and taken into captivity. Jerusalem would be destroyed.)
3. How might the original readers have felt if God ended the book at 3:8? (Afraid, disheartened, thinking that God had just cast His people away from Him.)
4. What encouragement would the Jews receive from Zephaniah 3:17 and surrounding verses? (Although God was disciplining His children, He still loved them. This would have given them hope.)
5. What special encouragement can we find in Zephaniah 3:17? (God consistently loves us; nothing will persuade Him to change His mind.)

Thank God in conversational prayer for His love and encouragement.

Week Three / Motion It In

Create your own hand motions to help you memorize Scripture. Here are some suggestions from Zephaniah 3:17. "The Lord (make a triangle representing the Trinity by touching your thumbs and two index fingers) your (point to a person) God (point upward to heaven) is with

you (point to a person), He is mighty (flex your biceps or pretend you are lifting weights over your head) to save'' (cross your arms in a figure of the cross).

Agree together on motions for the rest of the verse, and practice them. Then compare your motions with those depicted above. Later, review by doing the motions silently, one person at a time.

Any verse or Bible portion can also become a prayer of thanks, help, or confession. Instead of just reciting a memory verse, pray it.

Zephaniah 3:17 might sound like this: "Thank You, Lord, for being my God and always being with me. Help me to rely upon Your mighty power when I am tempted. Thank You for rejoicing over me with singing and for loving me in spite of myself. Help me to believe and trust You."

Consider these three key questions for application of your memory verse:

- What does God want me to *know*?
- How does He want me to *feel*?
- What does He want me to *do*?

Don't get discouraged if you learn the verse today and can't remember it tomorrow. Instant recall comes only through constant repetition over many weeks. But once you've grasped a Bible portion, it will take less review to keep it fresh in your mind.

Week Four / Keeping It Going

Review your memory verse by writing the first letter of each word. When a verse has more than one sentence or thought, it helps to write each segment on a separate line. Zephaniah 3:17 looks like this:

Z 3 1 7.
T L Y G I W Y,
H I M T S.
H W T G D I Y,
H W Q Y W H L,
H W R O Y W S.
Z 3 1 7.

On another occasion, have each member draw doodles for each word or phrase in the memory verse. Here are some examples from Zephaniah 3:17. "The Lord your God (draw a triangle labeled T.L.Y.G.) is with you (draw stick figures around your triangle), He is mighty (draw a man's flexed bicep) to save" (draw a cross). Make your own sketches before showing your family the example on page 33.

Develop a family plan for Bible memorization, deciding how much you want to have learned by a specific date. Then break your goal into bite-sized pieces.

For example, you may want to learn ten verses related to salvation during a ten-week period. Memorize one verse each week. Or maybe you'd like to memorize an entire book in a year. For a small book, like Philippians,

you would need to learn only two verses a week. Memorize a continuous passage without the verse numbers.

Many people consider one or two verses a week a good, steady diet. Ask the Lord to show you how much Scripture He wants you to memorize. And pray about your new venture daily, depending on the Holy Spirit to give discipline and remembrance.

Here are some suggested salvation passages to memorize:

- Fact of sin—Romans 3:23
- Penalty of sin—Romans 6:23
- Christ's payment—Romans 5:8
- Salvation a free gift—Ephesians 2:8–9
- Receiving Christ personally—John 1:12
- Assurance of salvation—John 5:11–13

You may prefer a passage dealing with another topic. Read the following chapters, and select appropriate portions for your family:

33

- Anxiety or worry—Philippians 4
- Family conflicts—James 4
- Fruitfulness in Christ—John 15
- Guidance—Proverbs 3
- Inferiority—Psalm 139
- Problems you didn't cause—Hebrews 12
- Spirit-filled life—Romans 8
- Success as a Christian—Matthew 5–7
- Temptation—Romans 6–7

Have you considered enrolling as a family in a Bible memory program? For more information, write to one of the following organizations:

Bible Memory Association
P.O. Box 12000
St. Louis, MO 63112

Moody Correspondence School
820 N. La Salle Drive
Chicago, IL 60610

From *The Poetic Interpretation of the Psalms* (Miracle Press, 1974).

MAY

Put WOW! into Bible Study

Reading and studying Scripture is commended and commanded by God (1 Timothy 4:13; 2 Timothy 2:15; Revelation 1:3). But sometimes Bible study can be more discouraging than delightful. Many people think they have mental Teflon, where nothing sticks, or detached retinas, seeing words without comprehending them.

Use this month's suggestions to broaden your Bible reading methods and strengthen your ability to retain God's Word. Ask the Lord to make time in His Word a satisfying experience for you and your family.

Week One / Where Loyalty Leads

Using your Bibles, decide together where you can find:

1. Zerubbabel
2. Paul's journeys
3. Building of Solomon's Temple
4. David's kingship
5. Abraham and Isaac
6. Ten Commandments
7. Crossing the Red Sea

8. Beatitudes of Jesus
9. Resurrection of Lazarus
10. Sermon on the Mount

If this quiz is too difficult, scramble the answers for a matching quiz. (Answers are at the end of the chapter.) The goal is to build motivation for the following techniques.

Read Esther 1. If your family includes younger children, use a simple Bible version or storybook. You may want to restate the narrative in your own words. Teens can read the chapter silently. A plain Bible text without annotations or summary headings will work best.

Suppose you were to find this chapter in a newspaper article. What would be an appropriate four- or five-word headline? Individually, determine the biggest ideas or activities of this chapter. Feel free to read or skim the passage again. Then create your own headline, and share it with the group.

Be specific. The word *disobedience*, for example, is too general; other Bible chapters deal with the same subject. Record your summary title in the margin of your Bibles or somewhere in your spiritual growth notebooks. (I titled Esther 1: "Proud King Banishes Queen!")

On another day, read Esther 2, and write a headline. (I chose: "Esther Wins Miss Persia Contest!") Based on the first two chapters, discuss what advice Esther might have given us from her own experience. Perhaps she would have said, "Be loyal to those who are over you, and God will reward you."

Webster defines *loyal* as "faithful in allegiance to one's lawful sovereign or government; faithful to a private person to whom fidelity is due; faithful to a cause, ideal, or custom." (You may need to define some words in this definition.)

Form two teams, and have them search in Esther chapters 1 and 2 for answers to their assignments.

Team one: How many examples of loyalty can you find? What were some of the results?

Team two: How many examples of disloyalty can you find? What were some of the results?

36

Team two: How many examples of disloyalty can you find? What were some of the results?

Team one might discover that: (1) Since princes were loyal to their king, the king took their advice on two occasions (1:10–22; 2:1–4); (2) Esther was loyal to Mordecai and to Hegai (2:7, 10–11, 20; 2:8–9, 15), so she was chosen to be queen of Persia (2:16–18); (3) Mordecai was loyal to the king and later promoted (2:21–23; chapter 6).

Team two might discover that: (1) Queen Vashti publicly disobeyed her husband (1:12), so he deposed her and looked for a replacement (1:19, 22); (2) two door-keepers plotted against the king's life, so they were both killed (2:21–23).

How did your family members display loyalty this week? Brainstorm together and make a list. What were the results of such loyalty? Mention at least one example of disloyalty that exacted a penalty. On a scale of one to five, evaluate your loyalty as a family to God, the government, society, church, and each other. "One" would mean "always disloyal," and "five" would represent "always loyal."

Has God's Spirit dealt with this subject recently in your family? Has there been a growing burden, uneasiness, or conviction about some response or attitude you need to change? Choose one area to improve as a family this week. Make it something specific.

You may want to show loyalty to the pastor by attending midweek services. Giving 10 percent of all family earnings could suggest loyalty to God. You might decide to refrain from sharing anything negative about family members with outsiders. Obeying traffic laws would demonstrate loyalty to the government.

Discuss how each person can contribute to the desired change and what benefits he or she will reap. Be sure everyone agrees with the decision; then hold one another accountable during the week. Don't forget to ask God for His help. Seal your battle plan by singing or reading together "Trust and Obey."

Share progress reports on your family goal from last week. Decide whether to continue with the same goal or select a new one.

Next, write headlines for Esther 3 and 4. For variety, read both chapters out loud, dividing the verses among family members. You could mark the text for different voice parts, depending on who is speaking or how the action changes. You might assign a narrator or have two or more people read in unison.

"What principles does God teach here?" This is an excellent applicational question for any Bible chapter. Scriptural principles are lessons for life. The following are some examples from Esther. See how many more you can find in chapters 3 and 4.

- Positions of authority may involve honor (3:1–2).
- In conflicts between human and divine law, God's commands should always be obeyed (3:2–4).
- Questions about motives should precede judgment about another's actions (3:3–4).

We can't always draw principles from a single verse; sometime they arise from whole paragraphs or chapters. For example, from Esther 3 we could conclude, "One person can affect the destiny of an entire society." Although we won't find these words in the chapter, they are impelled from the context. In such cases, look for similar ideas taught clearly in other Bible passages. (Compare Proverbs 14:34; Genesis 17:1–9; and Romans 5:17 with Esther 3.) Also consult cross-references or a topical Bible. Your own headlines will eventually help you compare Scripture with Scripture.

Pair younger and older members. From Esther 3 and 4, discover specific ways one person influenced others. See who can find the most in five minutes.

Possible answers include: (1) By not bowing before Haman, Mordecai caused the king's servants to become curious about his faith (3:2–4); (2) Haman wrongly used his position to secure the king's decree and almost destroyed the Jewish people (3:8–11); (3) Mordecai mourned, and his fellow Jews throughout the land followed his example (4:1–3); (4) Mordecai also persuaded Esther to use her new position and plead with the king for her condemned race (4:6–16).

Discuss what influence family members have on one another. Think of a personal illustration in which you influenced someone else, either positively or negatively, and share some of the consequences. As a group, consider your family's impact on neighbors, merchants, employers, teachers, relatives, or others you contact regularly.

Praise God that He works through His children to influence others. Thank Him for people He has used to strengthen your family life. Tell Him how anxious you are to obey Him, ask for sensitivity with those you encounter, and make yourself available as an instrument of righteousness. Read Romans 6:11–16.

Week Three / Ask the Right Questions

Curiosity and questioning help us get more from our Bibles. This week, write original headlines to summarize Esther 5, 6, and 7. Then pretend you are detectives looking for clues about the following topics and make notes about what you find. Try dividing these topics among older family members to research, or assign them over several days.

Characters: Who are the characters mentioned? (Esther, King Ahasuerus, Haman, Mordecai, Haman's friends and wife, Zeresh, the king's eunuchs, and Harbonah.

Who is the major human character? What do we learn about him or her? (Esther—she strategically interceded for her people before the king. Or Haman—his selfishness backfired more than once.)

Events or ideas: Some Bible chapters recount events (characters doing something); others reflect ideas (someone delivering thoughts). Esther 5–7 mainly contains events. List them. (Esther approaches the king, 5:1–4; he

39

and Haman enjoy her first banquet, 5:5–8; Haman brags to his friends and complains about Mordecai, 5:9–14; the king decides to honor Mordecai, 6:1–10; Haman accomplishes the king's command, 6:11–13; Esther presents her petition, 6:14–7:6; Ahasuerus's anger burns, and Haman is hanged 7:7–10.)

Places: Where does the action occur? See chapter 1. (King Ahasuerus reigned from India to Ethiopia over 127 provinces. Esther held her banquets at their home in Susa, the capital; 1:1–2.) Locate significant countries and cities on biblical or secular maps. Or read about them in a Bible dictionary.

Summary verse: Select one or two verses from each chapter to sum up the section (possibly 5:4 or 5:9; 6:6 or 6:10; 7:6 or 7:9).

Summary words: Choose one or two key words to summarize each chapter. (Chapter 5—golden scepter, banquet; chapter 6—honor; chapter 7—petition, gallows.)

Similarities: Can you find repeated words or phrases? Are any ideas or events alike in some way? Use the following questions to help you see similarities in Esther 5–7:

1. How many banquets did Esther prepare? (Two, 5:5 and 6:14.)
2. Three times the king made a promise to Esther. What was it? (To give her up to half his kingdom if she wanted it, 5:3, 6, and 7:2.)
3. What three requests did Esther make? (Twice she invited the king and Haman to a banquet, 5:4, 8. She also asked the king to spare her life and the lives of her people, 7:3.)
4. What one event did King Ahasuerus finally acknowledge? (Mordecai saved the king's life by reporting two servants who planned to kill him, 6:2–10; cf. 2:21–23.)
5. How many commands did the king issue? (Four: an announcement to attend Esther's banquet, 5:5; a

statement ushering Haman before the king's presence, 6:5; the command for Haman to honor Mordecai, 6:10; the edict to hang Haman on his own gallows, 7:9.)

Contrasts: Also notice differences and comparisons. These clues suggest some contrasts in Esther 5–7.

1. What event in chapter 5 made Haman glad, and what angered him? (The queen wanted to honor him at a banquet, vv. 8–9; Mordecai didn't respect or fear him, v. 9.)
2. What one thing did Haman come to discuss with the king, but the king had another topic in mind? (Mordecai's execution, 6:4. Instead, they talked about honoring Mordecai, 6:6–10.)
3. Who thought he would be honored, and who actually received honor? (Haman thought it, 6:6; Mordecai received it, 6:11.)
4. What contrasting news did Haman share with his family and friends? (The queen found favor with him, 5:12; Mordecai was honored instead of Haman, 6:10– 13.)
5. In what different situation would Esther have remained silent? What made her speak? (She would have stayed quiet if her people were simply sold into slavery, but they were also destined to die, 7:4.)
6. Something made the king furious. What appeased his anger? (He found out that Haman was a traitor, and it looked as if this man was even accosting the queen, 7:5–8; only hanging Haman on the gallows he had prepared would make the king's anger subside, 7:10.)

Applications: How can we implement these chapters in our lives this week? It's important to jot down something specific we plan to do in response to God's Word and ask His help to follow through.

For example, we could apply what Esther herself learned. She discovered that her God was big enough to work out even apparently impossible situations. But first she had to cooperate with Him. The Lord may want to develop in us this same kind of gentle and humble spirit. Or He may use our proper responses to authorities to achieve His plan. If we humble ourselves, God can exalt us in due time (1 Peter 5:6).

Week Four / A Fun Way to Remember

Write headlines for Esther 8, 9, and 10 as you study these chapters this week. Then gather all your headlines for the entire book.

Read the following grocery list out loud: onions, watermelon, soup, flour, relish, eggs, and lettuce. Ask if anyone can repeat the list from memory. Then rearrange the list as an acrostic, forming the word *flowers*.

Flour
Lettuce
Onions
Watermelon
Eggs
Relish
Soup

Note that an acrostic uses each letter of a vertical word to start another word or thought. Practice reciting the list once or twice and notice how much easier it is to remember.

Learning our chapter headlines will help us recall what we have read in the Bible. But an acrostic will enable us to remember Scripture in sequence. Brainstorm for a list of possible ten-letter themes describing the book of Esther, so you have one letter per chapter. (Perhaps "Jews Spared," "Haman's Plot," or "Persian Jews."

Choose one phrase and work through your Esther headlines to form an acrostic. Be careful not to stretch meanings or violate the chapter's context. You'll want to grab a thesaurus for possible synonyms.

Drill each other on your original Esther acrostic. Give a small prize to the first person who can correctly recite it from memory. A few days later, after further review, test your memories with the following list of events. Ask for volunteers to cite the appropriate chapter.

- Haman gets approval to destroy all Jews (3).
- Jews arise victorious over their enemies (9).
- Haman leads Mordecai through the city to honor him (6).
- Esther is chosen as queen (2).
- Esther says, "If I perish, I perish" (4).
- The Feast of Purim begins (9).
- Queen Vashti is removed from her position (1).
- Mordecai asks Esther to intervene for her people (4).
- The king has Haman hanged on the gallows (7).

One couple, Barry and Linda Huddleston, completed the whole Bible in sixty-six acrostics, chapter by chapter. Their results were later published in a book called *The Acrostic Bible.** Note the sample from Esther using the theme "Purim Feast" (chapters are in parentheses).

Persian decrees against Vashti (1)
Uncle Mordecai saves king (2)
Revenge plotted by Haman (3)
Intercession made to Esther (4)
Making the dinner for Ahasuerus (5)

Favor shown to Mordecai (6)
Esther requests her life (7)
Ahasuerus promotes Mordecai (8)
Sons of Haman hanged (9)
Testimony to Mordecai's greatness (10)

Barry says that tilting the Bible's chapters and forming them into acrostics brought him more joy and drew Him closer to the Lord than anything he's done with Scripture. Ask God to help you enjoy Him and His Word more.

---

*You can secure *The Acrostic Bible* at a Christian bookstore or from Media Ministries, 516 East Wakeman, Wheaton, IL 60187, for five dollars postpaid.

Read Psalm 119:1–24. What words indicate the psalmist's excitement about God's Word? Do we share his viewpoint?

Choose a Bible book you want to read next to make chapter headlines. Consider one that is being taught at church. It's best to pick a short book and to design an acrostic as a separate project *after* tilting the chapters as accurately as possible. Otherwise, there's the danger of forcing a chapter to fit whatever letter you need next.

Answers to quiz for Week One:

1. Ezra 2-5
2. Acts 13-28
3. 1 Kings 6
4. 2 Samuel 1-24
5. Genesis 11-18

6. Exodus 20
7. Exodus 14
8. Matthew 5
9. John 11
10. Matthew 5-7

JUNE

Reliving Joshua's Battles

God has revealed Himself to mankind in written words and through the living Word, His Son. The communication cycle is incomplete, however, until His message is received, understood, and applied. God didn't give His Word simply to satisfy our curiosity about ancient peoples and cultures, but to make us like Christ.

This month's family Bible activities will help us become more sensitive to words God uses in His Book and encourage us to respond with greater understanding and obedience.

Week One / Gaining Courage

Use the following crossword puzzle to summarize the content of the Book of Joshua. Clues for the puzzle are embedded in the story line, which is divided among four weekly sessions. But you may prefer to solve the entire puzzle in one or two sittings.

Make photocopies for older children, teens, or adults to work individually. Consider a reward for the one who correctly finishes first—such as a day off from household chores, breakfast in bed, or each family member doing one special favor for the winner.

These clues are based on the *New American Standard Bible.* You'll find answer locations and any appropriate Bible verses in parentheses. For example, (84-A; 1:2) indicates that the answer to 84-across may be found in Joshua 1:2. (The answer key is at the end of the chapter.)

After the death of Moses, the Lord's (84-A; 1:2), God spoke to (4-A; 1:1), the (61-D; 1:1) of (8-D; 1:1). God commanded him to (6-D; 1:2) and lead the sons of (78-A; 1:2) across the (24-D; 1:2; 4:1) River. They were about to (60-A; 1:11) the (17-D; 1:11) that God was giving them.

"(26-A; 1:5) man will be able to stand before you. . . . Only be (1-A; 1:7) and very (13-A; 1:7); be careful to do according to all the law . . . (20-D; 1:7) you may have (1-D; 1:8) wherever you (21-D; 1:7). This (43-D; 1:8) of the (37-A; 1:8) shall not depart from your mouth, but you shall (32-D; 1:8) on it day and night . . . then you

46

will have (1-D; 1:8)." Joshua urged the people to (64-D; 1:13) the Lord. (83-A; 1:17) the people had obeyed Moses, (27-A and 69-A; 1:17) they promised to (71-D; 1:17) Joshua in all (67-D; 1:17). Anyone who (10-D; 1:18) should be killed.

As you read Joshua 1:1–9, place an exclamation mark in your Bible margin beside every command God gave Joshua. (Commands are in verses 2 and 6–9.) Draw a happy face next to each encouragement God gave. (Note verses 2–9.) Use a pencil, not a pen, so it won't soak through your Bible pages or smear before drying. Colored pencils work well.

At a later time, mark other passages in Joshua with these symbols:

- Rainbow for blessings and promises
- Pitchfork for sins
- Trumpet for prophecies

- Open book for God's laws
- Sword for battles
- Triangle for God's character
- Footprint for steps of obedience

Draw the symbols on a piece of thin cardboard, or place a piece of carbon paper under this page to trace them. Then cut out the symbols with an X-acto knife or single-edge razor blade. Use this as a template when needed.

Now, as a family, discuss the following:

- Why did God tell Joshua so many times to be strong and courageous?
- What could have made Joshua fearful? (Perhaps he didn't know how to lead the Israelites now that Moses had died; maybe he wondered if the people would accept his leadership. He also had to face enemy nations.)
- Name something that might cause you to be afraid this week. What encouragement can you draw from Joshua 1 to strengthen you spiritually?
- Match one of God's attributes to each family member's need. (For example, if someone has a big decision to make, it helps to remember that God is all-knowing.)

Thank God for His consistent encouragement, and make every effort to be obedient to Him this week.

Week Two / A Sermon in Stones

Joshua (65-A; 2:1) two (62-D; 2:1) to the city of (33-D; 2:1), where they lodged at the (76-A; 2:1) of (74-D; 2:1), who said, "Give (18-A; 2:12) a pledge." God assured Israel they would conquer these peoples: (28-D; 3:10), (49-A; 3:10), (30-A; 3:10), and (85-A; 3:10).

When Israel crossed the (24-D; 4:1) River, Joshua commanded the priests to (80-D; 4:5) memorial stones and set them up (83-D; 4:19) Gilgal. They ate produce of Canaan that (82-A; 5:12). Joshua lifted up his (19-A; 5:13) and met the captain of the Lord's host with a drawn (51-D; 5:13) (42-A; 5:13) his hand.

With Bibles open to Joshua 4, see which family member is first to find the correct answers to the following questions.

1. How many piles of stones were made? (Two.)
2. Where were the stones placed? (One pile in the Jordan River and another where the Israelites camped.)
3. How many stones were in each pile? (Twelve.)
4. What was the significance of the number? (One for each of the twelve tribes of Israel.)
5. What was the purpose of the stones? (To be a memory aid for the Israelites.)
6. For whom were they especially intended? (The Hebrew children.)
7. What would the stones accomplish? (Arouse the children's curiosity and cause them to ask their parents what the stones meant.)
8. What were the parents to say when their children asked about the stones? (vv. 6–7, 21–24)

What other memory aids has God given His people in Scripture? Take turns portraying several. One person should silently act out the answer while the rest of the family tries to guess. He can only shake his head to indicate yes or no for every question or suggested answer. Then tell why the symbol was important.

The list includes:

- Sabbath day—God is our Creator.
- Animal sacrifices—Old Testament saints needed them to approach God, who is holy.
- Rainbow—God will never again destroy the world with a flood.
- Passover—the Israelites were delivered from Egyptian captivity.
- Pillar of cloud/pillar of fire—God was present as He led His people.

- Ten Commandments written on stone—God gave Israel His law.
- Baptism—Christian believers are identified with Jesus by faith.
- Communion—Christ's body was broken and blood shed for our redemption.

List some specific things God has done for your family and thank Him together. Then brainstorm for memory devices to remind each person of God's faithfulness. Choose one or two to implement this week.

Week Three / The Wall Drama

After the Israelites marched around (33-D; 6:2) seven (31-D; 6:4) on the seventh day, the walls fell (34-D; 6:20). Israel lost thirty-six (12-D; 7:5) at (35-D; 7:5) because of the sin of (35-A; 7:1). Joshua mourned until (63-D; 7:6). Joshua gathered the people on Mount (9-A; 8:33) and Mount (66-D; 8:33) to read the (37-A; 8:32) of Moses and to (75-D; 8:33) the people. The people of (70-A; 9:3) deceived Joshua, who had to let them live (79-A; 9:20) wrath be on Israel. Joshua later (14-D; 10:6) them. God made the (7-A; 10:13) stand still for Joshua to capture five kings (48-A; 10:17) Makkedah and (46-A; 10:18) (12-D; 10:18) (56-A, 50-D and 58-D; 10:18) guard them.

Joshua gave Hebron to (29-D; 14:13). Not all the (47-D; 13:2–3) were conquered; some Anakim remained in (81-A; 11:22).

For younger children, read or tell how Jericho was conquered by Joshua and the Israelites (Joshua 6). Make the account as vivid as you can; your audience should listen carefully, so they can act out the story afterward.

Discuss what the Hebrews might have looked like and how they felt walking silently around the great city walls. What are some comments the people of Jericho might have made during that week?

Let everyone take a part, regardless of age. Babies, for

example, can crawl around "Jericho." Someone else might portray Rahab inside the city.

Old towels, sheets, robes, and shirts make good costumes. Cardboard from large appliances or furniture can be used for city walls. But let your family's imagination be the main props.

Next, decide the moral of the story. You may want to stress that God can give us victory over seemingly impossible situations if we respond in obedience.

In which difficulties today would we like God to work a miracle? What steps of faith and obedience might we first have to take? Choose one "Jericho" to trust God to overcome this week. Determine how each family member must respond and commit the situation to God.

Only the tribe of (55-D; 13:14) did not get a land inheritance. The two-and-a-half tribes who received land (59-D; 12:8) the (45-D; 15:5) side of the (24-D; 4:1) were: (2-D; 13:15), (41-D; 13:24), and (11-D; 13:7). A city of Gad was (72-D; 13:25). The nine-and-a-half tribes dividing Canaan according to (57-A; 15:1) were: (33-A; 15:1), (39-A; 16:8), (11-D; 17:1), (44-A; 18:11), (15–A; 19:1), (16–A; 19:10), (86–A; 19:17), (68–D; 19:24), (52–A; 19:32), and Dan. Part of Asher's territory was (77-D; 19:30). Judah's border on the south was (63-A; 15:21), and one of its towns was (73-A; 15:50). Caleb's daughter got her (38-D; 15:18). One of Manasseh's families was named (54-A; 17:2). One girl in Manasseh had the famous name of (3-D; 17:3). The (22-A; 21:41)s were given forty-eight cities with their accompanying pasture (25-A; 21:41). One of their cities was (9-D; 21:21).

When Joshua was very old, he gathered Israel at (7-D; 24:1) to remind them that they were not to turn (68-A; 23:6) from God's (37-A; 23:6) to the (40-D; 23:6) or the left. They were to serve God with all their (36-D; 22:5). It was (5-D; 24:7) who had (53-D; 24:3) them from Egypt. The people had (29-A; 24:22) to serve the Lord. After his farewell messages to Israel, Joshua died at the age of one hundred and (23-D; 24:29).

Lay out an imaginary map of Canaan on your family room or living room floor. Place furniture pieces to represent the Sea of Galilee, Jordan River, Dead Sea, and coastline of the Mediterranean Sea. From a Bible map distinguish where each of the twelve tribes of Israel settled. Label pieces of cardboard with the tribal names and work together to arrange them in their relative locations on your floor map. If you have enough people participating, let individuals represent the tribes.

Older children can research an assigned tribe, using a Bible dictionary or concordance. What important Bible characters, if any, came from that tribe and what significant events took place in its territory?

Trace an outline map of Israel in Joshua's time for younger children to color with crayons.

Read Joshua's farewell speech (chapters 23 and 24) aloud after selecting one of the following topics to note and discuss.

- What miracles did Joshua call to the people's remembrance? What did he say God desired to do for them? What does God want to accomplish in and for us if we trust and obey Him?
- What sins did Joshua warn the people against? What would be the consequences if they disobeyed God? Are we experiencing any consequences because of our own sinful behavior?
- What promises did the Israelites make to Joshua and to the Lord? Did they keep their word? (Skim the first three chapters of Judges for the answer.) What promises have we made to God, and have we fulfilled them?

Thank God for His unfailing faithfulness.

To review the story of Joshua, read out loud all four sections of crossword puzzle clues. Let family members guess each missing word.

Something to think about: If you were to give a farewell speech to your family, what would you say?

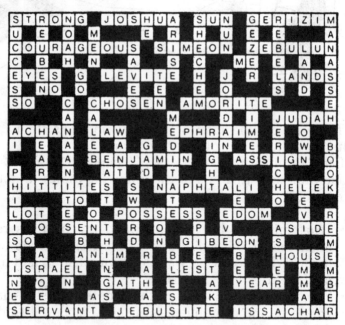

JULY

God's Kind of Love Overshadows Ours

How do we know if we're doing a good job at work? We compare our performance with the job description. One of our main "jobs" as Christians is loving others. Read Matthew 22:37–39 and John 13:34. Ask a dozen people what they think it means to do a good job loving people. You'll probably get many different replies.

In the Bible's love chapter, 1 Corinthians 13, we find God's job description for perfectly expressing His love to others. Although fifteen characteristics are presented in this passage, we'll discuss the first four. Split the suggested sessions according to your family's schedule and attention spans.

Begin by copying 1 Corinthians 13:4–7 onto an index card. Carry it with you daily to memorize love's true job description.

Week One / Love Is Patient

How do you know when another person really loves you? Brainstorm for a list of qualities. Why is simply saying "I love you" not sufficient?

55

How do we know God loves us? (He tells us so in the Bible and proves it by His actions.)

What is God's love like? Read 1 Corinthians 13:1–8 in an easy-to-understand translation, such as the *New International Version*.

Ask each family member to answer the following questions privately with "always," "usually," "sometimes," "usually not," or "never." You don't need to share results, but each person should become motivated to improve weak areas.

1. Am I patient?
2. Am I kind?
3. Do I envy others?
4. Do I brag about myself?
5. Am I proud?
6. Am I rude?
7. Am I self-seeking?
8. Am I easily angered?
9. Do I keep track of wrongs?
10. Do I like to do evil things?
11. Do I love the truth?
12. Do I protect others?
13. Do I trust people?
14. Do I hope for the best in people?
15. Do I keep on loving?

For questions one, two, and eleven through fifteen, give yourself ten points for each "always," eight points for each "usually," six points for each "sometimes," two points for each "usually not," and no points for each "never" answer. For questions three through ten, give yourself no points for each "always," two points for each "usually," six points for each "sometimes," eight points for each "usually not," and ten points for each "never" answer.

If your total score is:

150: You are in a near state of perfection.
130–49: You are doing fantastic, with a little room for improvement.

110–29: You are coming along fine, with lots of room for improvement.

90–109: You have some leanings in the right direction, but a long way to go.

Less than 90: Well, there's hope for anyone who wants to do better. With God all things possible.

Work together to match each question to one of the scenes in the picture collage on page 57.

God's kind of love is *patient.* The Phillips version of the New Testament says "slow to lose patience," and the King James Version says "suffereth long." The phrase originally meant "long-tempered with the idiosyncrasies of others." Look up *idiosyncrasy* in a dictionary. Then discuss as a group what bothers you about others. Why are some people so hard to get along with? Why do we become impatient with certain people? Don't bring up pointed or personal comments. Instead, finish the phrase: "I can't stand the way people—"

Have younger children look through coloring books for illustrations of patience, such as Charlie Brown's willingness to kick the football though Lucy has pulled it away countless times. Parents may want to select one or two examples for the children to color.

How long are we to be long-suffering? Read Peter's question about this in Matthew 18:21. How many times did Peter think was sufficient for forgiving another person's shortcomings? (Seven.) What was Jesus' answer in verse 22? (Seventy times seven.) How much is seventy times seven? (Four hundred ninety.) If we forgave someone once a day, how long would it take us to use up 490 days' worth of forgiveness? (About one year and four months.)

But how do we lengthen our patience fuse? By counting to ten before we blow up? Try thanking God for His patience with us. Even more than earthly parents, our Heavenly Father continually cherishes those who have been born again into His family through faith in Christ's sacrifice. Help each member remember the many times God has forgiven him.

Older children may be interested in figuring out how long God waited during the days of Noah for the people to repent. (About one hundred twenty years, 1 Peter 3:20; Genesis 6:3.) How long has Jesus waited to return to the earth? (Almost two thousand years.) Why such a long delay? Read 2 Peter 3:9. (God is giving each person time and opportunity to accept His gift of eternal life.)

Look up the words *patient* and *patience* in a concordance or topical Bible. Find references to Bible characters who exhibited patience, such as Joseph in prison or Job with his trials and "comforters." Study their examples for principles we can apply to our own lives.

Read Philippians 1:6. How long will God forgive His children? (Until we are fully redeemed and safely in His presence.) Write Lamentations 3:22–23 on both sides of a card and stand it in the center of your dining room table. Now encourage each family member to thank God for His patience with him or her.

Then thank one another for your patience with each other.

Week Two / Love Is Kind

Open this week's meeting with nominations for "The Kindest People We Know." Include a reason with each name: "I nominate (name) because—" Make a composite list, and after each name jot down one or more examples of the person's kindness.

Discuss what common denominator each nominee shares. Kindness means looking for ways of being constructive, useful, profitable, and encouraging to others. Why doesn't this quality come naturally? How can we become kinder?

Read Galatians 5:22–23, and note that kindness is a fruit of the Holy Spirit. What significance do you see in the word *fruit* being singular? (The fruit of the Spirit is a cluster; a kind person will also exhibit love, joy, peace, patience, goodness, faithfulness, gentleness, and self-control.)

Let each family member make a card or note for one or

59

two people on the list. Guide a young child's hand to sign his or her name. Notes should be simple, such as: "Tonight, our family was thinking about the kindest people we know. I nominated you because you volunteered to fix my bike tire. And anytime you see me you wave and say hi. Thank you for making my world a nicer place to live."

Suppose someone gave you a small amount of money to spread love and kindness into the lives of others. What would you do with it?

Have older children work with younger ones to stimulate ideas and estimate costs within an allotted amount. They should choose less expensive items or activities in order to brighten the lives of the most people. A big bag of candy, for example, can be shared with everyone on the school bus. Or teachers might like personal appreciation notes written on special stationery.

If possible, distribute funds and carry out your family's suggestions. For teens, the exercise will be more meaningful if they have to earn the money or take it from their allowance. You may prefer brainstorming for ideas that don't cost anything, such as helping with homework, carrying something, repairing an item, being a good listener, or asking someone for prayer requests.

Put each family member's name on separate pieces of paper, and have everyone draw one. For the next seven days, be extra kind to the person you chose. Ask the Lord to help you be creative. Remember the meaning of kindness: "constructive, profitable, useful, and encouraging." Be sure to keep the person in suspense until it's time to reveal yourself.

Read 2 Corinthians 8:9 and Romans 5:8 to learn how God shows His kindness to us. Ask the Lord to flood your heart with His fruit today, since kindness is a matter of the heart.

Can you name individuals who are smarter than you? Live in a bigger or nicer house? Have more friends? Own more pets or toys? Drive a better car or ride a more expensive bike? Make or have more money? Are more talented?

Names will probably come easily. Regardless of who we are or what we do, there always seem to be those who have it nicer or can do things better.

Now go through the above list again, this time thinking of people you know who could answer your name to some of the questions. Does anyone believe you are smarter, live in a nicer house, or have more friends? Discuss why we focus on those we think are above us.

What's our attitude when we hear of others with better report cards? How do we respond when a friend tells of his promotion, when we overhear another person being complimented, or when we're defeated in a school election or contest?

Involve your family in an impromptu dramatization of James 2:1–4 and 14–17. Let one person be a church usher who shows favoritism. The others can arrive for a service either well-dressed or poorly-dressed. The usher should make the well-dressed people feel welcome, while ignoring or disdaining the others.

One of the poor can claim to have no wood for his stove and no food for dinner. Have the usher or other well-dressed church officer say, "Go, I wish you well; keep warm and be fed," but not offer any help. Then another person should preach a message from James 2:1–17 to the rest of the family.

Afterward, ask the role players, "How did the poorer ones feel toward the richer ones?" and, "How meaningful are nice words without actions to match them?"

True love does not envy. The original idea behind the word *envy* is "to boil or be hot because of jealousy" or "to have a strong affection toward something." Envy is a spiritual cancer that feeds on our thoughts and grips our emotions. As a cooperative project, design a colorful

61

poster to illustrate the caption, "Don't allow the kettle of envy to simmer, for it will easily come to a boil!"

Discuss the role that modern media plays in creating dissatisfaction with what we have and are. Think of some recent examples of television viewing that changed or created some desires in family members.

Take a walking tour in and around your home. Record items that were once greatly desired but are now neglected or in disrepair. Decide who might be thrilled to receive some of the items. Make necessary repairs and personally give the items away.

One antidote to the green-eyed monster is to recognize that God has given each of us gifts and abilities to please Him and do His will. Make a list of your assets—personal qualities, possessions, relationships, and skills. Have other family members add suggestions to one another's lists. Open drawers and doors, if need be, to make corrections or additions.

Ultimately, all our gifts come from God (James 1:17). What have we brought into this world, and how much can we take out of it? See Job 1:21. Thank God for each item on your assets list, and ask Him to remind you not to be envious this week. Periodically, share your progress with the rest of your family.

Week Four / Love Does Not Boast

Read the following poem to your family:

> Whenever Richard Cory went downtown,
> We people on the pavement looked at him.
> He was a gentleman from sole to crown,
> Clean favored, and imperially slim.
> And he was always quietly arrayed.
> And he was always human when he talked;
> But still he fluttered pulses when he said,
> "Good morning," and he glittered when he walked.
> And he was rich—yes, richer than a king.
> And admirably schooled in every grace;
> In short, we thought that he was everything

To make us wish that we were in his place.
So on we worked and waited for the light,
And went without the meat, and cursed the bread.
And Richard Cory, one calm, summer night,
Went home and put a bullet through his head.
(Edwin A. Robinson, *The Children of the Night*)

Make a composite description of Richard Cory as he might have appeared in your community. Why did others envy him? How much did his admirers really know about him? What is the folly of judging a person by external appearance? What are some possible reasons Richard Cory took his life?

God's kind of love is not "anxious to impress" others (1 Corinthians 13:5, Phillips). Drawing undue attention to ourselves can be vainglorious, meaning "empty glory." If we perform good deeds conspicuously to catch the praise of men, we'll miss our Heavenly Father's reward. Discuss the following questions from Matthew 6:1–18.

- Who is Jesus warning us not to be like? (Hypocrites or play-actors.)
- In what ways did the hypocrites boast or try to make an impression? (They sent trumpeters to announce their charity, prayed on busy street corners, and disfigured their faces so people would know they were fasting.)
- What deeds should we do secretly? (Give to the needs of others, pray, and fast.)
- Contrast the reward of the hypocrite with that of the person who isn't out to impress others. (The former doesn't get a reward from God—recognition and praise of men is his sole reward; the latter is rewarded openly by God.)
- What common ways do people in our society try to impress others? (Stretching the truth about their accomplishments, overdressing for an occasion, living beyond their means, talking too much about themselves or the successes of their family members.)

Together, pray through the disciples' prayer from Matthew 6:9–13. What truths in this passage help us avoid being boastful? (Only God's name is worthy of honor and glory; we are citizens of a heavenly kingdom who desire God's will over our own; our daily bread comes from God; we need forgiveness from God and should in turn forgive others; only God can deliver us from temptation and Satan's influence.)

What promise does 1 Peter 5:6–7 have for us? (If we humble ourselves, God will exalt us at the right time.) Plan good deeds for other family members this week and secretly do them.

AUGUST

At Home with Love

Everyone needs to love and be loved. In our homes, love is the glue God designed for uniting diverse personalities, the oil for smoothing interpersonal relationships, and the honey for sweetening life.

Read 1 John 4:10–21. God not only commands us to love one another, but He also demonstrates and describes true love. Let's continue to study such characteristics from 1 Corinthians 13:4–7. The Bible clarifies how to choose loving attitudes and actions.

Week One / Love Is Not Proud

How would your family describe an unloving person? Brainstorm together for two minutes while someone records the responses on a chalkboard or large pad of paper. Then read 1 Corinthians 13:4–7, a phrase at a time, from a modern version. Contrast Paul's list of what a loving person is like to your own. Then restate each characteristic in Paul's list as an opposite.

Using J. B. Phillips's translation, for example, an unloving person will:

- Be quick to lose patience (have a short fuse)
- Not look for ways to be constructive
- Be possessive (jealous or envious)

65

- Be anxious to impress (boast)
- Cherish inflated ideas of his own importance (be puffed up with pride)
- Have poor manners (be rude)
- Pursue selfish advantage (insist on rights)
- Be touchy (be easily provoked or angered)
- Keep account of evil (review wrongs)
- Gloat over the wickedness of others (rejoice at injustice and unrighteousness)
- Be unhappy when truth prevails
- Have no trust in God or people
- Have no hope (any semblance of it fades under contrary circumstances)

Thank the Lord that His kind of love is the opposite to all of the above. Ask Him to fill you with His Spirit and His love.

Now focus on the fifth phrase, love "is not proud." Find a dictionary definition of *pride* and see how other translations handle 1 Corinthians 13:4.

What is at the center of the words *pride* and *sin*? (The letter "i".) One random survey monitored five hundred telephone conversations and counted 3,990 references to self. During dinner some evening, stop anyone who uses the word "I" and have him restate his thought. See who can last the longest without using the word.

Ask yourselves the following questions to check for the problem of pride. Allow time to reflect silently on each.

1. Am I more self-centered or other-center?
2. Do I expect life to revolve around me?
3. Do I admit when I am wrong?
4. Do I ever volunteer to be someone's servant?
5. Am I flexible when I relate to others?
6. Do I always have to be right?
7. Do I talk more than I listen?
8. Can I ask for help when I need it?

Now consider Isaiah 14:13–14 in light of Luke 10:17–18. How many times did Satan use the word "I"? (Five times against God.) What did he want? (To take God's place in heaven.) Pride cost Lucifer something, according to Isaiah 14:12, 15. What was it? (His privileged position among the angels.)

Have someone read Genesis 3:1–6. Ask the group to decide how Satan's prideful attitude in Isaiah 14 was reflected in the serpent. (The snake challenged what God said; he made Eve feel the Lord was not good.)

See who can find any consequences of sin in the rest of Genesis 3. Don't overlook self-consciousness (v. 7), fear and withdrawal (v. 10), and passing the blame (vv. 12–13), as well as those in verses 14–19. Older teens might want to study Genesis 4 to discover how Lucifer's prideful attitude was reproduced in Cain and his descendants.

For each day this week, write one of the following passages with its accompanying question on an index card. As a group, discuss possible answers the following day.

- Psalm 73:1–9. Why should we never envy proud people?
- Proverbs 16:5, 18. Why are proud people more likely to stumble?
- Proverbs 26:12. Why is there more hope for a fool than for someone who is wise in his own eyes?
- Hosea 7:9–10. Why does persistent pride lead to folly?
- Mark 7:21–22. Why is pride listed with sins like murder and adultery?
- 1 John 2:15–17. What is the source of pride, and where does it lead?

God hates pride because it opposes His kind of love. When we're too self-sufficient, we can neither receive help from others nor help them with their own needs. Discuss the remedy for pride implied in 1 Corinthians 4:6–7. All we are and have is from God. What attitude should the truth of James 1:17 instill in us? (Gratitude.)

Sing or read together these words from a well-known hymn.

When I survey the wondrous cross,
On which the Prince of Glory died,
My richest gain I count but loss,
And pour contempt on all my pride.

Week Two / Love Is Not Rude

Have each family member complete the sentence, "A person is rude when he or she—"

Being rude implies practicing poor manners—doing what's inappropriate to the situation. The word translated "rude" in 1 Corinthians 13:5 (NIV) literally means "following the instincts of nature."

As a group, try to summarize good manners in one word. (Thoughtfulness, appropriateness, courtesy, tact, sensitivity, refinement—all these help grasp the concept.) What would you call a person who has good manners without love? (Perhaps a snob.) Can a person ever truly love without good manners? (According to this verse, no.)

Let's see how well our expectations have been communicated and met. Ask each child to list three to five manners most pleasing to his parents. At the same time, parents list manners most desired. Then compare lists, and discuss any differences.

Repeat the procedure, this time asking what manners children desire in their parents. Have every member choose one or two manners to work on this week. Adopt a special signal to use when someone fails to use the agreed-upon manner. Discuss the question: Why do we sometimes display our worst manners toward those we love the most?

Another evening this week, have a model dinner when everyone will practice his best manners. As you discuss the experience afterward, agree on a composite list of "Ten Commandments for Table Manners." Be sure to state them positively.

Later, encourage each family member to make a personal place mat of these ten commandments. For a challenge, depict them without words, using stick fig-

ures or magazine photographs. With younger children, outline pictures for them to color. Cover the finished art with adhesive-backed clear plastic.

Read and discuss about five verses each day from Ephesians 5:1—6:4. Teens and adults may also want to read the gospels of Mark or Luke, which emphasize the human side of the God-man. Note examples of Christ's good manners. Ask the Lord to make each family member more like Jesus in this respect.

Week Three / Love Is Not Self-Seeking

The media encourage self-centeredness. Advertisers create in us dissatisfaction with what we possess. And our world's philosophy shouts: "Watch out for yourself, because no one else will."

From a pile of newspapers and magazines, have your family select examples of ads that appeal to our selfish nature. Ask questions to help everyone see through the veneer of those advertisements.

Read and discuss Matthew 6:19–34. What are some problems we encounter when we focus on the accumulation of things? What does Jesus command us to seek instead? What does this passage teach about God's knowledge of us? How does He care for us? What's wrong with using this passage to abandon all interest in seeking material needs?

From the following, choose several questions or activities that will meet your family's needs and interests:

- Discuss why we can't gain lasting satisfaction through accumulating things. Skim Ecclesiastes, and list Solomon's attempts to find satisfaction apart from God. Note his conclusion in chapter 12.
- Other than God, what are the only eternal entities in the world today? (God's Word and people: Luke 21:33; John 5:24, 28–29). How does selfishness block relationships between people?
- What impact should the truths of 2 Peter 3:9–12 and 1 John 2:15–17 have on our view of material goods?
- According to 1 Peter 5:8, who is seeking you and for what purpose? List some of Satan's goals for you.
- According to Luke 19:10 and John 4:23, who else is seeking you? What are His goals? Consult 2 Peter 1:2–8; Galatians 5:22–23; and 1 Corinthians 13:4–7.
- Do you agree or disagree with the statement: "You can make more friends in two months by being interested in others than you can in two years by trying to get others interested in you?"

Week Four / Love Is Not Easily Angered

What causes fights in your home? Think of a time when family tempers flared, but be determined not to restart the argument. What personal rights were involved?

Discuss some of the rights or freedoms we must yield to live in an orderly and civilized society. (For example, driving my car at any speed I wish, not paying taxes, or building whatever I want on my city lot.) What are some of the potential consequences for the person who doesn't choose to relinquish these rights?

List some of the rights we must yield to live in harmony in our homes. (Loud music, odd practice times, our own curfews, or talking on the telephone for hours.) What are some benefits of yielding such rights or the consequences of clinging to them regardless of others?

When we become angry, often it's an indication we feel one of our rights has been violated. But is anger legitimate? See Exodus 32:1–10 and Mark 3:5. The key to righteous indignation depends on whose rights have been violated: ours or another's.

What do you consider your "rights?" In a prayer of dedication, offer them to God as a gift. Realize He may take some away temporarily or permanently.

We sometimes find it hard to believe God is both all-loving and all-powerful, which inhibits us from yielding our rights and possessions. Meditate on Psalm 139,

asking yourself: How much does God know about me? Does He have my best interests at heart? Can God carry out His good intentions? Can I trust Him with my relationships, possessions, and dreams?

From Philippians 2:1–11, determine the rights Jesus was willing to lay aside to become a man and our Savior. Using Philippians 3:4–16, list what rights Paul gave up to become a Christian and a missionary. What were some of Jesus' and Paul's rewards?

Read Romans 5:8 and John 15:13. Praise the Lord for being willing to die for you; tell Christ you want to live in appreciation of His sacrifice, surrendering all rights to Him.

Brainstorm for a list of your parents' selfless attitudes and acts in bringing you into the world and raising you. Using pictures cut from magazines, make a collage card to send to them, expressing appreciation for their sacrifices.

Thank God for placing you in His choice of the best family for you.

SEPTEMBER

Pardon Me, but Your Attitude Is Showing

If you want to change your garden's harvest from corn to beans, it won't be sufficient to hang beans on the cornstalks. The corn must be uprooted and beans planted in its place.

Vegetation's identity is revealed by what it produces. What is at the root determines the fruit.

The same is true of people—attitudes determine actions. A tongue's "bucket" can only deliver what it gets out of the mind's "well." Outer reformation must begin with an inner transformation (Romans 12:1–2).

At the heart of the matter is the human heart. That's why 1 Corinthians 13 begins by describing the necessity of possessing God's love within us (vv. 1–3) and then tells us how love should appear when practiced in our life-styles (vv. 4–7).

Let's ask the Lord to help us demonstrate our gratitude to Him and to others with loving attitudes—followed up by actions.

Week One / Love Keeps No Record of Wrongs

Set a timer for two minutes in order to brainstorm. Compose a list of things God *cannot* do (for example:

sin, deny Himself, act contrary to Scripture, abandon His children, change His character, and so on).

Ask individuals to read these passages and from them state things God cannot do:

- Psalm 139:1–6 (God can't learn anything about us; He knows it all already.)
- Hebrews 8:12 (God can't remember forgiven sin.)

What do we learn about God in Psalm 103:10–12? (He is merciful, loving, and forgiving.) How far East do we have to go before we are West? (We can't get there that way. True East and West go off into infinity on a straight line.)

How does a dictionary's definitions of *forget* help us to understand how God, who knows everything, can forget our confessed sins?

Pretend you are detectives looking for clues in 2 Samuel 12 to show that God held no grudge against David for his crimes with Bathsheba. (God allowed David to marry her; God loved their next child, Solomon, sending presents and a nickname; God allowed Solomon to be the next king.)

Why do you think 1 Chronicles, God's later commentary on David's life, makes no mention of David's sin with Bathsheba? (God forgave him and forgot it.)

What's wrong with this attitude: "I can forgive him, but I can't forget what he has done"? (Such a person hasn't really forgiven.)

What does it mean to forgive someone? (Jot down responses.) What do dictionary definitions of *forgive, excuse* (verb), and *pardon* add to a proper understanding of forgiveness?

What can we learn about forgiveness from the way God forgives us? (He forgets the offense and treats us as though we had never wronged Him.)

What does the last phrase of 1 Corinthians 13:5 teach us about true love? (It keeps no record of wrongs. "Keeping account" is a bookkeeping term, used to set down a permanent record of one's debits and credits so they won't be forgotten. Here it means to store up memories of wrongs received.)

Demonstrate how a checkbook register is used. What would God consider to be our debts? (Sins.) Where can we get credits against our sins that God will accept? (See 2 Corinthians 5:21.) Read Romans 4:5, which uses the same original word as 1 Corinthians 13:5. If we believe in Christ, what does God put into our account? (Righteousness).

Optional activity for older members: Read Ephesians 1:3–14 and list in a "ledger" other good things God has put down to the believer's account. A report could be given to the family.

According to Hebrews 6:10, what can't God forget? (The good we do. He keeps a careful record of it.)

Make a family "bank book" (notebook) with a separate account (page) for each member. Appoint a "family banker" to keep records of only good deeds done by family members for one week. The deeds listed cannot

be mentioned by the person who did the deed; others must notify the banker. Treat the largest account holder to a double portion of his or her favorite dessert. Vote by secret ballot to see if members wish to open new accounts for another week.

Optional: Older teenagers may wish to keep private ledgers to record both debit and credit entries of their own attitudes and actions.

What's wrong with holding a grudge against someone, especially if they did us a great wrong? (Nursing a grudge will poison your mind, sour your disposition, make you think everyone has bad motives, and close the door to patching up a friendship.)

To what extent do we control our memories? (To remember something, we have to go over it again and again; we choose what we mentally replay.)

Have each member who can make a copy of these questions for personal meditation:

- Do I have any evidence against another that I need to destroy?
- Do I need to make any apologies?
- Am I holding on to any matters that I should bury deep and consider gone forever?

Week Two / Love Does Not Delight in Evil

Make a rule that for one meal a day only good news may be shared. Later discuss:

What travels faster—bad news or good news? Why?
Can we escape hearing about sin?

List the sources through which your family receives most of its news about people and events. (Be specific in listing newspapers, television programs, magazines, conversations, and "grapevines.") On a scale of zero to five (with zero always being negative and five always being

76

positive), rate the kind of input generally received from each source of news. Then figure an overall average for your family's "IQ" (Input Quotient).

Discuss ways to decrease negative input and increase positive input.

Optional for young teens: Select some media examples that glorify evil. Discuss some of the possible consequences of sin that are missing in the ads or articles.

"Guesstimate" what percentage of today's conversations pertain to people. Is it mainly good or bad news that is shared about people? Why do others' weaknesses often make for more interesting conversation than their strengths? (Sometimes it is to make ourselves appear better in comparison.)

What is gossip? Look it up in a dictionary. Then put the definition into your own words. (Sharing personal information with people who are neither part of the problem nor part of the solution.) How do we know gossip is not an act of true love? (Love doesn't delight in exposing the sins of another; rather it seeks to protect others' interests and promote their welfare.)

According to 1 Corinthians 13:6, what should we never delight in? (Evil—injustice and unrighteousness.) J.B. Phillips says that loves does not "gloat over the wickedness of other people."

The word *delight* or *rejoice* reflects the most common Greek word for greeting other people. We are not to greet evilness with gladness. We are not to welcome news about the sins and shortcomings of others.

Which of the following are proper reactions to news of another Christian falling?

- Secretly feeling it serves him right
- Praying for his restoration
- Trying to restore him in the spirit of meekness
- Seeking all the details under the guise of "being better able to pray for him"
- Enlisting "prayer support" by sharing the story
- Believing it must be true, even if we don't hear it directly from the source

Why should we never rejoice over the downfall of an enemy? (See Proverbs 24:17–18.)

Optional for older members: Look up the word *buzzard* in an encyclopedia. How is a person who gossips like a buzzard?

What can we do to make conversations focus more on positive things? (Discuss ideas, aspirations, feelings about events; speak only positively about people; be interested in the one with whom we speak.)

Ask the Lord to give you creativity, love, wisdom, and boldness to stem the tide of unwholesome conversation.

Do we share *good news* as often as we can? What good news can we spread? (The word *gospel* means good news.)

Create a newspaper using all the good news you can uncover in your neighborhood or community. Creatively include some good news from God. Make photocopies of your paper for friends and neighbors.

Read or sing together this prayer by Frances R. Havergal:

> Take my lips, and let them be
> Filled with messages for Thee.
> Take myself, and I will be
> Ever, only all for Thee.

Week Three / Love Rejoices with the Truth

Use scrapbooks or photos to relive some past family outings. Discuss how each experience might have been different if you were there all alone.

What does 1 Corinthians 13:6 say we should not do? (Delight in evil.) And what *should* we do? (Rejoice with the truth.) Phillips translates the last part of this verse: "It [love] is glad with all good men when truth prevails." The Greek word used means "to rejoice together." We should congratulate others and take part in their joy.

Conduct a Bible search for things we can rejoice in, using these passages: 2 Chronicles 6:41; Psalm 13:5; 31:7; 35:9; 97:1; 118:24; 119:162; Proverbs 5:18; Ecclesiastes 5:18; Luke 10:20; 15:3–10; Romans 12:15; 1 Corinthians 12:26; Philippians 4:4. (You could use a Bible concordance to find others.) Make a list of results, and praise God in prayer or song for each one.

For younger children, use a few of these passages to play charades or "twenty questions." (In twenty questions, members may ask only yes and no questions about one thing you rejoice in. If no one guesses within the twenty-question limit, tell the answer and take another turn. If someone guesses correctly, that person selects a new subject of rejoicing and answers the other's questions.)

Meditate on these questions:

- Can I accept my family members as they really are?
- Is my love limited in its endurance?
- Can I live with the inconsistencies of others?
- Can I trust the Holy Spirit to convict others, or do I always have to point out their faults?

79

Here is a suggested personal or family prayer: "Lord Jesus, I want to be loyal to the people You have brought into my life. Please help me focus on their good traits and patiently bear with their weaknesses. And please help them to do the same with me."

Use shelf paper to make a few banners with large-lettered words from some of the above passages. Hang them prominently around the house. For a few days, require family members to recite one of the banners for admission to the dinner table. (It must be a different verse each time, and, obviously, with no peeking.)

According to Deuteronomy 30:9, Isaiah 65:2, and Zephaniah 3:17, what does God rejoice in? (Us—His people.)

Think about how much (or how little) you enter into rejoicing or suffering with others outside your family circle.

Week Four / Love Always Protects

What would you do if you were a photographer and a friend who had a birthmark on one side of his face asked you to take his portrait? (Focus on the side without the mark).

The Living Bible expands the thought of 1 Corinthians 13:6–7: "If you love someone you will be loyal to him no matter what the cost. You will always believe in him, always expect the best of him, and always stand your ground in defending him."

What four things does true love always do (v. 7)? How do different Bible versions translate the first one? (Always protects; bears all things.)

The original word literally means "a roof" or "a proper covering."

Think of some ways God protects us. (Be sure to include that He keeps to Himself most of what He knows about us.)

Imagine putting a shield of love around yourself so a cutting remark or unfriendly attitude won't wound your spirit. How might we put a protective shield around others? (Bear what we learn about them on the wings of prayer to God rather than on the wings of words to men.)

Do we have to tell all we know? Why is it a mark of mature love to weigh the effects of our words before we speak them?

Why is it better not to make a hurting comment than to make one and ask forgiveness afterward? (The memory of those words can linger for life.)

Form two "listening teams," then have one member read James 3. One team should listen for illustrations of the power of our tongues; the other for James's suggestions on how to tame our tongues.

In conversational prayer, ask forgiveness for the misuse of our tongues and dedicate them to the protection of others.

OCTOBER

Test Your Biblical IQ

To many believers, Bible study is like trying to work a gigantic jigsaw puzzle without access to a completed picture on the puzzle box lid. It can be frustrating to never see the panorama, just lots of small pieces.

This month's quizzes and Bible-learning activities are designed to help you put some of the familiar Bible pieces in perspective with the big picture. The adult's and children's quizzes each summarize the Scripture story with fifty blanks for you to complete. You may prefer to do the Old Testament questions from both quizzes in the first week and the New Testament questions during your second week.

Just for fun, there is a Bible riddle for you to solve—all it needs is one simple answer!

The Bible book word search puzzles can be done anytime. Try to locate the names of all sixty-six Bible books. Answers may be found forward or backward, horizontally, vertically, or diagonally. Hint: Some answers share letters. The original puzzle was developed by Dan Zachary. The answer key is on page 97.

Give yourself four points for each correct answer on either quiz (children's or adult's) for week one or two.

BIBLE BOOK NAMES SEARCH

```
S T C E N S I S N A M O R E T H C L O U J D B V
N N J F Y E R A G S S I W Q K U T E B O Z O N M
A H O M S E F E I G L P C U H X E I H A J O H D
I B S I B T D W V O N S N A I H T N I R O C K N
N E H M T E X U D E M O I G H Q U A O N P W A Y
O F U S R A S E J U L M M O P P E D O Y E C L H
L N A W E S T H E R E A B E H T C M G A X O O T
A R O U N M C N O R L Y T A Q Z O X F H O P I O
S H A M O C A J E A S E I I W L L A B S D T C M
S D E A E E S J C M R D Y M O N O R E T U E D I
E Z E K I E L H C Y A L K S O N S T A S S E H T
H M U N S P I L K B Z L F A E R S H D U V I N N
T L E U M A S S O L T O B C H A I A S I J W M O
O N A H L U T P I N G S N A I T A L A G X O W M
Z E C H A R T P H N G N U S A G N E I C I C E E
E E B M S B V T O I R Z E P H E S I A N S I H L
P O C U P L A S T C L L D U S N J O N A G O T I
H M L H J E S K S U C I T I V E L H A B N O T H
A C D A A K T R K C W T P V F S K A A X I Q A P
N T E N O R L D E U T E A P Y I E B O N K U M E
I A G G A H I B A K K U R H I S B R E V O R P D
A R Z A G G L A F R W V Z C O A S E G D U J A Y
H U S W E R B E H A I M E H E N N O I T G R A M
J X E P S U S L C H R O N I C L E S H D E S M E
```

Then compare your score with a standard grading scale at one Bible college:

94–100 A (for Above the rest)
87–93 B (for Better)
80–86 C (for Common or average)
70–79 D (for Do try harder)
0–69 F (for Find more time to study your Bible)

A correct answer to the following riddle gives you the satisfaction of knowing you are a genius!

A Bible Riddle

God made Adam out of dust,
  but thought it best to make me first;
So I was made before the man,
  according to God's most holy plan.
My whole body God made complete,
  without arms or hands or feet.
My ways and acts did God control,
  but in my body He placed no soul.
A living being I became,
  and Adam gave to me a name.
Then from his presence I withdrew,
  for this man Adam I never knew.
All my Maker's laws I do obey,
  and from these laws I never stray.
Thousands of me go in fear,
  but seldom on the earth appear.
Later, for a purpose God did see,
  He placed a living soul in me.
But that soul of mine God had to claim,
  and from me He took it back again.
And when this soul from me had fled,
  I was the same as when first made;
Without arms, legs, feet, or soul,
  I travel on from pole to pole.
My labors are from day to night,
  and to men I once furnished light.

Thousands of people both young and old,
   did' by death bright lights behold.
No right or wrong can I conceive;
   the Bible and its teachings I can't believe.
The fear of death doesn't trouble me;
   pure happiness I will never see.
And up in Heaven I can never go,
   nor in the grave or hell below.
So get your Bible and read with care;
   you'll find my name recorded there.

(Author Unknown)

Week One / The Scripture Story for Children

After answering some of these questions, use the references included with the answers (listed below) to read
from the Bible about any missed or unfamiliar people or
events. You may wish to apportion the questions throughout the week and intersperse them with other family
activities. See January—Week Three for suggestions for
using Bible questions while playing a game.

Prepare applicational questions about a few of the
items below. With number nine, for example, you might
ask, "How do we know that Abraham loved God with all
his heart?" (He was willing to give God his only son.) Or
with number six, "Why did only eight people ride in
Noah's boat?" (Everyone was warned about the great
Flood, but most people chose not to believe God's
preacher.)

Ask God for sensitivity to your family's attention span
and level of spiritual interest.

The world's first parents, (1) _____ [man] and (2) _____
[woman], lived in a beautiful garden called (3) _____
[place]. A (4) _____ [creature] talked them into disobey-
ing their Creator.

The first child ever born was (5) _____ [name], who
later killed his brother (6) _____ [name]. Finally people
became so wicked that God told (7) _____ [name] to
build a big boat called an (8) _____ [thing]. Only eight

people were saved, while the rest of the world was destroyed.

Most of the Old Testament is about the Hebrew people. Some of their famous leaders are remembered for unusual things, such as:

(9) _____ [name], who nearly sacrificed his son on an altar.

(10) _____ [name], for his coat of many colors.

(11) _____ [name], for being in a basket among the reeds as a baby.

(12) _____ [name], who marched around the city of Jericho until the walls fell down.

(13) _____ [name], for testing God's will with a fleece and conquering the Midianites with clay pitchers that covered burning torches.

As history, continued, some of the Hebrews set world records, such as:

(14) _____ [name], for slaying one thousand Philistines with the jawbone of a donkey.

(15) _____ [name], who killed a lion and a bear all by himself.

(16) _____ [name], for being the wisest and wealthiest man in the world.

(17) _____ [name], for starting a fire with wet wood on Mount Carmel.

(18) — [name], who survived a night in a den of hungry lions.

There are (19) _____ [number] books in the Bible, with (20) _____ [number] in the Old Testament and (21) _____ [number] in the New Testament. The first seventeen books of the Bible are about God's people from creation to the close of Old Testament history. The remaining Old Testament books tell about people who lived then and events that happened during that time.

Book of poetry follow the history section, starting with a man named (22) _____ [person], who suffered the loss of his family and possessions. The longest book of the Bible is (23) _____ [book] with one hundred and fifty chapters. Wisdom to help us make the right choices is found in the next book, which is (24) _____ [book].

The Old Testament closes with books of major and

minor (25) _____ [category], divided according to their size. Some of these writers had unusual experiences, such as:

(26) _____ [name], who saw the Lord in His holy Temple and said, "Here am I; send me."

(27) _____ [name], who wrote an eye-witness account of Jerusalem being destroyed.

(28) _____ [name], who saw wheels within wheels as well as a valley of dry bones.

(29) _____ [name], who rode inside a great fish for three days.

The New Testament is about Jesus and His apostles. The first four books in order are: (30) _____ (31) _____ (32) _____, and (33) _____ [books]. These books are sometimes called (34) _____ [category], meaning "good news."

Jesus' birth was announced to His mother by the angel (35) _____ [name]. Jesus was born in (36) _____ [city] and was worshiped by (37) _____ [a group] and later by wise men. Because King (38) _____ [name] wanted to kill Jesus, He was taken to (39) _____ [country] and later returned to grow up in (40) _____ [city].

Jesus often taught in stories or parables. Some were about:

A man called the (41) _____ [title], who helped someone who had been beaten and robbed on the road to Jericho.

A good shepherd who left ninety-nine (42) _____ [animals] to find one.

A boy called the (43) _____ [title], who ran away from home into a far country, lost everything, and was later welcomed home by his father.

Jesus also did miracles to help His disciples believe He was God. Some of them were:

Walking on the water of the Sea of (44) _____ [place].

Raising His friend (45) _____ [name] from the dead.

Raising Himself after being (46) _____ [type of death] for our sins.

The fifth book of the New Testament, (47) _____ [book], records Jesus' ascension and sending His disciples into the world as witnesses. Jesus' followers who set records included:

(48) _____ [name], who died as the first martyr.

(49) _____ [name], who traveled the most miles on missionary journeys.

(50) _____ [name], who became the first missionary doctor.

Letters to churches and Christians fill up the remainder of the New Testament. The book of Revelation describes Jesus' return to the world in power and glory.

Answers for "The Scripture Story for Children"

1. Adam (Genesis 2:20)
2. Eve (Genesis 3:20)
3. Eden (Genesis 2:15)
4. Serpent (Genesis 3:1)
5. Cain (Genesis 4:1)
6. Abel (Genesis 4:8)
7. Noah (Genesis 6:13–14)
8. Ark (Genesis 6:14)
9. Abraham (Genesis 22:1–2)
10. Joseph (Genesis 37:3)
11. Moses (Exodus 2:3, 10)
12. Joshua (Joshua 6:2–3, 5)
13. Gideon (Judges 6:36–37; 7:15, 20)
14. Samson (Judges 15:14–15)
15. David (1 Samuel 17:34–36)
16. Solomon (1 Kings 3:10–13)
17. Elijah (1 Kings 18:31–38)
18. Daniel (Daniel 6:16–22)
19. Sixty-six
20. Thirty-nine
21. Twenty-seven
22. Job (Job 1:13–21)
23. Psalms
24. Proverbs (Proverbs 1:1–7)
25. Prophets
26. Isaiah (Isaiah 6:1–8)
27. Jeremiah (Lamentations 1:1–8)
28. Ezekiel (Ezekiel 1:3, 15–21; 37:1–10)

29. Jonah (Jonah 1:17)
30. Matthew
31. Mark
32. Luke
33. John
34. Gospels (Mark 1:1)
35. Gabriel (Luke 1:26–33)
36. Bethlehem (Luke 2:4–7)
37. Shepherds (Luke 2:8–20)
38. Herod (Matthew 2:13)
39. Egypt (Matthew 2:13)
40. Nazareth (Matthew 2:19–23)
41. Good Samaritan (Luke 10:30–35)
42. Sheep (Luke 15:4–7)
43. Prodigal son (Luke 15:11–32)
44. Galilee (Matthew 14:22–34)
45. Lazarus (John 11:41–45)
46. Crucified (John 19:17–18; 2:19–22)
47. Acts (Acts 1:7–11)
48. Stephen (Acts 7:55–60)
49. Paul (Acts 13–21)
50. Luke (Colossians 4:14; Acts 1:1–4)

Answer to Bible Riddle: The great fish that swallowed Jonah

Week Two / The Scripture Story for Adults

If your family includes younger children, you may want to use some of the questions from week one at this time. Or give increasingly simple (or more specific) clues for the desired answer. For example, use these hints for the answer to number 4:

• A famous man from the Bible
• An ancestor of Jesus
• God asked him to leave his country for a promised land
• This man was married to Sarah
• God later gave him a son named Isaac

- His name begins with the first letter of the alphabet
- The last three letters of his name is a type of meat from pigs

Again, plan some applicational questions.

After (1) _____ created everything, He sent judgment on a rebellious race through a worldwide (2) _____ [event]. He later separated the nations with different languages and scattered them from (3) _____ [place].

(4) _____, (5) _____, and (6) _____ [persons] were founding fathers of the Hebrew people. Sold into slavery, (7) _____ [person] became a powerful foreign leader. The Israelites developed into a great nation during (8) _____ [number] years in (9) _____ [country], until their deliverance from bondage. Then (10) _____ [person] led the people across the (11) _____ [body of water] and taught them God's law at (12) _____ [place]. (13) _____ [person] led the Israelites into their Promised Land after a (14) _____ [number] year trek in the wilderness because of unbelief.

The transition toward monarchy entailed about (15) _____ [number] years of fourteen deliverer-rulers called (16) _____ [group], the last of whom was (17) _____ [person]. The first three Hebrew kings, (18) _____, (19) _____, and (20) _____ [persons], each ruled forty years. Under (21) _____ [king] the Hebrew nation divided into Northern and Southern Kingdoms, respectively called (22) _____ [place] and (23) _____ [place].

After the reign of (24) _____ [number] wicked kings in the north, (25) _____ [country] conquered and scattered the Northern Kingdom. After the rule of (26) _____ [number] kings for about (27) _____ [number] years, the Southern Kingdom was taken into captivity by (28) _____ [country] for (29) _____ [number] years.

While (30) _____, (31) _____, and (32) _____ [persons] led Jews back to Jerusalem over a hundred-year period, (33) _____ [person] was a savior-queen in (34) _____ [country].

More than (35) _____ [number] "silent years" span the gap between Malachi and Matthew.

The New Testament opens with the births of (36) _____ [person] and Jesus, the latter through the virgin (37) _____ [person]. About (39) _____ [number] years later, (39) _____ [person] challenged the Jews to indicate their repentance by submitting to (40) _____ [ordinance].

God's incarnate Son publicly showed the world what God is like and taught His perfect ways for about (41) _____ [number] years. After preparing (42) _____ [number] disciples to continue His work in the world, Jesus died voluntarily on a (43) _____ [thing] for mankind's sin, rose from the dead, and returned to (44) _____ [place].

Later, empowered by the (45) _____ [person], the disciples spread the good news about salvation among the Jews. The apostle (46) _____ [person] carried the gospel to the Gentiles through (47) _____ [number] missionary journeys and wrote at least (48) _____ [number] New Testament letters. The section of our Bible from Hebrews through Jude contains (49) _____ [number] additional letters penned by five men. The apostle (50) _____ [person] recorded the Revelation, which summarizes God's final program for this world. The Bible ends as it began— with a new, sinless creation.

Answers for "The Scripture Story for Adults"

1. God (Genesis 1:1; 2:1–4)
2. Flood (Genesis 7:13–24)
3. Babel [or Shinar] (Genesis 11:1–9)
4. Abraham (Acts 7:8)
5. Isaac (Acts 7:8)
6. Jacob (Acts 7:8)
7. Joseph (Acts 7:9–10)
8. Four hundred [or four hundred thirty] (Exodus 12:40)
9. Egypt (Exodus 12:40)
10. Moses (Exodus 12:31–33)
11. Red Sea (Exodus 15:22)
12. Sinai [or Mount Sinai] (Exodus 19:1–7)
13. Joshua (Joshua 1:1–4)
14. Forty (Joshua 5:6)

15. Three hundred fifty [from about 1400 to 1050 B.C.]
16. Judges (Judges 2:7, 17)
17. Samuel (1 Samuel 7:15)
18. Saul (Acts 13:21)
19. David (2 Samuel 5:4)
20. Solomon (2 Chronicles 9:30)
21. Rehoboam (1 Kings 12:1, 16–19)
22. Israel (1 Kings 12:19–20)
23. Judah (1 Kings 12:19–20)
24. Nineteen
25. Assyria (2 Kings 17:5–6)
26. Twenty
27. Three hundred fifty [from 930 to 586 B.C.]
28. Babylon (2 Kings 25:8–12)
29. Seventy (2 Chronicles 36:20–21)
30. Zerubbabel (Ezra 2:1–2)
31. Ezra (Ezra 7:6–7)
32. Nehemiah (Nehemiah 1:1; 2:11)
33. Esther (Esther 2:17; 4:13–17)
34. Persia (Esther 1:1–3)
35. Four hundred [from about 425 to about 5 B.C.]
36. John [the Baptist] (Luke 1:5–17, 59–64)
37. Mary (Matthew 1:18–25)
38. Thirty
39. John [the Baptist] (Matthew 3:1–2)
40. Baptism (Matthew 3:5–6)
41. Three [or three and one-half; determined by number of Passovers mentioned]
42. Twelve (Mark 3:13–19)
43. Cross (John 19:17–18)
44. Heaven (Acts 1:11)
45. Holy Spirit (Acts 1:8)
46. Paul (Acts 18:5–6; Romans 11:13)
47. Three (Acts 13–21)
48. Thirteen (Romans through Philemon)
49. Eight
50. John (Revelation 1:1–4, 9–10)

Introduce this week's topic by asking family members to write the numbers ten through one in a descending column. Read the following ten clues slowly, allowing time for written answers after each one. The winner is the person who correctly guesses the answer at the highest number. Don't say the answer aloud until all clues have been read. Younger children may whisper their guesses to an older member.

Can you guess this Bible character?

10. Name shared by three men in the Bible
9. A captain of the Lord's army (Joshua 5:15; Hebrews 2:10, KJV*)
8. A shepherd (1 Peter 5:4)
7. A rabbi (John 6:25)
6. A king (Matthew 27:37)
5. New Testament equivalent to Joshua in the Old Testament
4. Name chosen by an angel for the baby before birth
3. Name means "Savior"
2. What an angel commanded Mary to name her first-born (Luke 1:30–31)
1. Begins with the letter J

(Answer: Jesus)

Can any member identify the three Bible men who share the name Jesus (Jesus Christ: Matthew 1:1; Joshua: Acts 7:45, Hebrews 4:8; Justus: Colossians 4:11.)

How many names or titles for Jesus can you find in Matthew 1:18—2:23, Luke 1:1—2:40, and John 1:1–18? (You may wish to select one passage and use the others later.)

Can your family think of Bible names for Jesus beginning with every letter of the alphabet? Compile your own list before reading the one below (which is not exhaustive).

*King James Version.

- Alpha (Revelation 21:6)
- Bread of Life (John 6:35)
- Christ (Luke 2:11)
- Day Star (2 Peter 1:19)
- Everlasting (or eternal) Father (Isaiah 9:6)
- Faithful (Revelation 19:11)
- God with us (Matthew 1:23)
- Holy One (Luke 4:34)
- Immanuel (Matthew 1:23)
- Jesus (Luke 1:31)
- King (Matthew 2:2)
- Lord (Luke 2:11)
- Messiah (John 4:25–26)
- Nazarene (Matthew 2:23)
- Only Begotten (John 1:18)
- Prince of Peace (Isaiah 9:6)
- Quick (Hebrews 4:12, KJV)
- Resurrection and Life (John 11:25)
- Savior (Luke 2:11)
- Truth (John 14:6)
- Unspeakable Gift (2 Corinthians 9:15)
- Vine (John 15:1)
- Word (John 1:1)

Give a special reward to any member who finds titles beginning with X, Y, or Z.

Encourage older children to help younger ones make an "ABC Scrapbook" with a page for each letter. Eventually add drawn or cutout pictures to illustrate words about Jesus beginning with each letter. Simple couplets could be homespun for each, such as, "Jesus is God become man; born to bring salvation's plan."

Older children can entertain themselves making a word search puzzle with the above list of names. Letter them onto a sheet of graph paper, with words running forward, backward, up, down, or diagonally. Keep a list of words actually used. Fill in any remaining squares with random letters before giving the puzzle to another to solve.

Sing or read "I Know of a Name."

Help each family member find the meaning of his

name. From its meaning, brainstorm one or more good spiritual goals for the person. For example, *Karen* means "pure one" and could serve as a motivation to think pure thoughts and resist temptations.

Ask Jesus to empower you to live up to your character goal.

Week Four / Heavenly Helpers

Again, ask members to record suggested answers beside the clue's number.

Can you guess this Bible character?

10. Existed before the earth was created (Job 38:4–7)
9. Spirit being who lives forever (Hebrews 1:13–14; Luke 20:36)
8. Helped answer Daniel's prayer (Daniel 8:16)
7. God's first spokesman in the New Testament (Luke 1:19)
6. Predicted two miraculous births (Luke 1:13, 19, 26–31)
5. Left a man speechless in the Temple (Luke 1:18–20)
4. Name means "Hero of God"
3. Told Mary she would be the virgin mother of Jesus (Luke 1:26–35)
2. One of God's angelic messengers (Luke 1:19, 26)
1. Begins with the letter G

(Answer: Gabriel)

Angels appeared six or seven times in connection with Jesus' birth. How many of these visitations can your family recall? Award a point for each correct answer to the person visited and the essence of the angel's message.

1. To Zechariah in the Temple about John's birth (Luke 1:5–22)
2. To Mary about the virgin birth of Jesus (Luke 1:26–38)

3. To Joseph about the virgin birth of Jesus to Mary (Matthew 1:20–23)
4. To the shepherds about Jesus' birth in Bethlehem (Luke 2:8–14)
5. To Joseph about taking Mary and Jesus to Egypt (Matthew 2:13)
6. To Joseph about returning to Israel (Matthew 2:19–20)
7. To Joseph about not returning to Judea (Matthew 2:22– 23; it's not certain an angel is involved)

See which member (or team) can find the most miracles performed by angels in the Bible passages listed above.

Use Hebrews chapter 1 to contrast angels with Jesus. Who do angels especially help (v. 14)?

Read together a Bible dictionary article about angels, or ask an older member to prepare a summary.

Ask younger ones to draw or describe their conception of an angel.

In conversational prayer, thank God for His angels and what they do in the world.

Read Hebrews 13:2. Make plans for entertaining a "stranger." Invite a single person or a senior citizen for dinner, and present him with a special gift from your family.

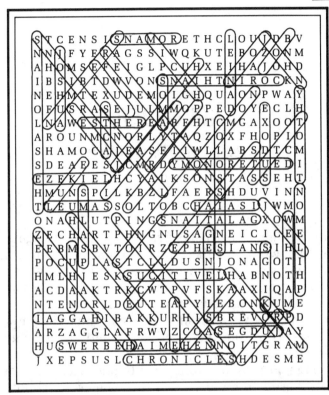

FOR

BIBLE BOOK NAMES SEARCH

NOVEMBER

A Psalm for Thanksgiving

Our thoughts at Thanksgiving are often thoughts of relief that we aren't like others: living in a politically oppressed society, starving in a famine-wasted land, missing limbs or normal abilities, fighting a debilitating disease, or driving a rusted and battered car.

True thanksgiving doesn't begin with human comparisons, but with God, the giver of life and all that's good (James 1:17).

Though Psalms is profuse with praise of God, only two of these one hundred and fifty poems are subtitled, "A Psalm of Praise." David wrote Psalm 145, and Jewish tradition ascribes Psalm 100 to him also. The unique Hebrew superscription of Psalm 100 is literally, "A Psalm for Thanksgiving."

The five short verses of Psalm 100 tell us why and how we can be thankful. The familiar King James Version is the basis for this month's study, but use whatever translation you have. Set a family goal to memorize this psalm during the next four weeks.

99

Read Psalm 100 aloud.

What three commands does God give us in Psalm 100:1–2?

What do you think God meant when He commanded His people to make a *joyful noise?* (To the Hebrews it literally meant "to shout for joy or blow the trumpets.")

What kind of joyful noises do football fans make when their favorite team has just scored a touchdown or won the game?

What kind of joyful noise should we make when God resolves a problem for us or answers our prayer? ("Praise God!" or "Thank you, Jesus!")

According to 1 Thessalonians 4:16, who will one day appear with a loud shout and trumpet blasts?

Read Revelation 19:6–7 aloud. With what words will God's children greet Him? ("Alleluia: for the Lord God omnipotent reigns. Let us be glad and rejoice, and give honor to Him.")

What phrase is repeated in every verse of Psalm 136? Divide into two groups to read this psalm aloud antiphonally, one side reading the first part of each verse and the other side answering loudly, "For His mercy endures forever."

For younger children, form a temporary rhythm band. Use a spoon and pan or two sticks for percussion instruments. Beat on each syllable of a simple song, such as "Jesus Loves Me" (which has seven syllables in each stanza line and a pattern of 5, 5, 5, and 6 in the four chorus lines). Read Psalm 150.

What words in the first two verses of Psalm 100 relate to our actions? Which words relate to our attitudes?

Why is gratitude to God a great motivation to serve Him? (When we consider all that God has done for us in Christ, the least we can do is serve Him.) How do you see this truth taught in Romans 12:1?

Serve (v. 2) literally means "to work as a slave." What was the apostle Paul's favorite description of himself (Romans 1:1)? (A bondslave to Jesus Christ.) Why does one's dedication to Jesus and His work in the world seem to be directly proportional to a person's sense of forgiveness?

Recall examples of times when proper service was nullified by an improper spirit. (Who likes to be served by a gloomy or grouchy waitress?) With what attitude should we serve God (v. 2)? (With gladness, literally glee or great rejoicing.)

In Genesis 29:20, what motivated Jacob to work gladly for his father-in-law, Laban? (His great love for Rachel, Laban's daughter.) Why doesn't a young man consider it work to wash his car for a date with a girl he's trying to impress?

How can we develop a deeper love for God? How can we show our love for our Savior (John 14:15; Matthew 25:40)? (Meeting the needs of others, no matter how small, counts as though it were given directly to Jesus.)

How does God want us to "come before His presence" (v. 2)? (With singing.)

According to Colossians 3:16, how can we develop our singing? (A song on the lips begins with Scripture in the head and a song in the heart.)

What motivated David to sing in Psalm 40:1–3? What was the theme of his song?

From Revelation 4:11 and 5:12, read part of a song God's children are singing in heaven. Then add your praises to God.

Memorize Psalm 100:1–2 aloud together. Review it often throughout the week.

Week Two / Our Great Shepherd

Review the first two verses of Psalm 100, and begin to memorize verse 3.

How many reasons for being thankful can you locate in verses 3–5? What do we learn about God in verse 3? About ourselves?

Look up Lord and God in a Bible dictionary. How do these names differ?

(Lord is "Jehovah," the self-existent or eternal one. God is "Elohim," the mighty One, the Creator God.)

By what name did God reveal Himself to Moses at the burning bush (Exodus 3:14)?

What relationship does God have with us in verse 3? (Creator and Shepherd.)

How does believing verse 3 make many miracles in the Scriptures easier to accept? (A God who can create human life can also heal disease, raise the dead, and preserve a prophet inside a great fish.)

How much faith is required to think that an eyeball "just happened"? That a pair of kidneys could evolve? That the more than five thousand mechanisms of the human body developed spontaneously? (It would take more faith than believing in God.)

What does the word creature mean? (A "created being.") Read David's prayer in Psalm 139:14–16, then look in a mirror, and rejoice in your Creator. Post a copy of Psalm 139:14 on a mirror as a reminder that we are not self-made.

What does it mean to "know God"? (Acknowledge who He is and give Him His rightful place in our lives.)

How do we become God's people? In what sense are Christians "twice God's?" (By creation and redemption.)

Who always takes the initiative to restore the broken relationship between God and His creatures? (God: Genesis 3:8–9; Luke 19:10.)

To "redeem" means to purchase as one's own possession. How did God purchase His Old Testament people? (By the blood of the Passover lamb; Exodus 13:13–15.) How are people redeemed today, according to 1 Peter 1:18–19?

Why can't God learn anything? (Because He knows everything.) How much did God know about us when He sent His Son to die for our sins (Psalm 139:1–12)?

What was David's occupation before he became a king? (Shepherd.) What famous psalm did he write about the Lord as our Shepherd? (Psalm 23.)

How much responsibility does a shepherd have for the welfare of his sheep? (Total.) Read Psalm 23, noting our needs that God will meet. Make your own observations before reading the following list.

If God is our Shepherd, we shall not want (lack):

- Rest and nourishment (vv. 1–2)
- Protection and refreshment (v. 2)
- Renewal and revival (v. 3)
- Direction and purity (v. 3)
- Peace amidst trouble (v. 4)
- Companionship (v. 4)
- Guidance and comfort (v. 4)
- Food and drink (v. 5)
- Joy (v. 5)
- Abundance to give (v. 5)
- Blessings (v. 6)
- Eternal life (v. 6)

Why is Jesus called the *Good* Shepherd in John 10:11? Why is He called the *Great* Shepherd in Hebrews 13:20? Why does Peter call Him the *Chief* Shepherd in 1 Peter 5:4?

Read or sing "Saviour, Like a Shepherd Lead Us" as a group prayer.

Week Three / Why Be Thankful?

Review what you have memorized from Psalm 100 so far. Work on memorizing verse 4 aloud together. Review the suggestions given for April if you need help in remembering Scripture.

How does Psalm 100:4 say we should approach God? What is the difference between *thanksgiving* and *praise*? (Thanksgiving focuses on what God does, and praise focuses on who He is.)

What hinders a grateful spirit in people? (Pride.)

Begin to keep a journal of gratefulness—a diary of what God does for you—with a goal of adding to it regularly.

What would you say to a person who doesn't feel thankful to God? (Perhaps ask: "Have you had air to breathe today? Lungs to exchange oxygen for carbon dioxide? Heartbeats to pump life-giving blood through miles of vessels to refresh millions of cells an average of seventy times each minute? Water to drink?")

Use the following references as a "sword drill," seeing who can locate each reference in his Bible the quickest. As each verse is read, note what gift from God is mentioned. Be selective if you have younger members.

Ephesians 1:3 (Acceptance in the beloved)
1 Peter 1:23 (Birth from above)
Colossians 2:10 (Complete in Christ)
Colossians 1:13 (Deliverance from darkness)
Ephesians 1:13–14 (Earnest of our inheritance)
Ephesians 1:7 (Forgiveness of sins)
Romans 12:6–8 (Gifts for service)
1 John 3:2–3 (Hope in heaven)
1 Peter 1:4 (Inheritance undefiled, and so on)
Romans 5:1 (Justification)
Revelation 1:6 (Kingship and priesthood)
John 10:10 (Life abundant)
1 Corinthians 12:13 (Member of Christ's Body)
2 Corinthians 5:17 (New creation)
Ephesians 2:18 (Open access to God)
Ephesians 1:19 (Power of God)
Ephesians 2:1 (Quickened by Christ)
Ephesians 1:7 (Redeemed by Christ's blood)
Ephesians 4:30 (Sealed by the Holy Spirit)
1 Corinthians 15:51 (Translation into heaven)
Romans 6:4–9 (Union with Christ)
1 John 5:4–5 (Victory in Jesus)
Ephesians 2:8–10 (Workmanship of God)
1 Peter 5:6–7 (eXaltation in God)
Revelation 20:6 (Years with Christ)
Hebrews 12:22–24 (Zion, our heavenly home)

What is unique about the way the above gifts have been listed? (They are in alphabetical order, with one for each letter—with a bit of tampering on "exaltation.") Brainstorm for other benefits God gives His children. Then thank Him specifically for them.

Sometime during this Thanksgiving week, create a homemade thank-you card for the Lord, expressing gratitude for all He means to you and has done for you. Read Psalm 103 if you need some specifics. Be sure to include contributions from every family member. Use the "postage" of prayer to "send" your card to heaven.

Plan a family thanksgiving and praise service in which each member has one or more parts.

Praise is a mild translation of a Hebrew word meaning "rave about or celebrate over."

As a group, list as many descriptive words about God as you can in three minutes. Add any of the following to your list: God is always-existing, all-controlling, all-powerful, everywhere-present, all-knowing, all-righteous, all-truthful, all-loving, and never-changing.

What should be our response to each characteristic of God? Be very specific with two or three of God's qualities. For example, because God is all-knowing, I can't hide anything from Him. I can't surprise Him, either, by anything I think or do. I should feel secure since He knows everything about me and still decided to love me, and so on.

Together memorize Psalm 100:5 aloud. Review the whole Psalm later.

How do *goodness* and *mercy* differ? (God's goodness gives us what we *don't* deserve; His mercy withholds what we *do* deserve.)

According to Romans 8:32, why should we never fear bringing our requests to God? What does Matthew 7:11 teach us about God's nature?

What does Peter say we should do with our cares (1 Peter 5:7)? The word CAST forms an acronym to recall four types of prayer:

- Confession: Agreeing with God about our shortcomings
- Adoration: Worshiping God for His attributes
- Supplication: Making ours or others' needs known to God
- Thanksgiving: Expressing gratitude for God's gifts

How balanced are these four topics in our prayers? Rephrase Psalm 103 aloud as a personal prayer. Other praise psalms suited to this method of worship are 104 and 144–150.

DECEMBER

Preparing for Christ's Birth

Advent is a time of preparation for Christmas. *Advent* means "coming and refers primarily to the coming of our Lord Jesus Christ into the world as a man."

An Advent wreath is used by many Christians for four Sundays (or twenty-four days) prior to Christmas to deepen their understanding of the Savior's birth.

This month we suggest planning family Bible times around an Advent wreath, a circle of evergreens with four or twenty-four candles, lighted progressively weekly or daily starting December 1 to symbolize the increasing brilliance of the prophecies regarding the Messiah's birth.

We've suggested activities for twenty-five days. If you opt for one weekly meeting, select from the week's activities.

You may make an Advent wreath by drilling candle holes in a circular board or by placing candles in a ring of modeling clay. Surround the base with Christmas greens, and treat evergreen boughs with a fire-retardant material. You may also dot the wreath with pinecones. Use medium or small candles, one close to your family's skin color and the rest purple. A large white candle may be added Christmas Day.

Family members may take turns lighting the candles, reading Scripture or hymns, and praying. If you don't have a hymnal, try to borrow one.

Week One / The Advent Wreath Pictures Jesus

Each session write one prophetic verse on a paper star to hang over the lighted candle with a long piece of string.

Day 1—Jesus is eternal (Micah 5:2; Hebrews 1:8)

What shape is the wreath? Can you find where the circle begins or ends? How is a circle like Jesus?

According to Micah 5:2, how long had Jesus been alive before He was born in Bethlehem? (From everlasting.) Locate Bethlehem on a Bible map.

What is Jesus called in Hebrews 1:8? How long will He rule the universe?

According to John 3:16, what kind of life will Jesus give us if we believe in Him?

Thank Jesus that He has no beginning or end. Ask Him to remind you of this when you see circles.

See who can count the most circles around the house. Give the winner a circle-shaped prize, such as a coin or scoop of ice cream.

Day 2—Jesus is the Light of the World (Isaiah 9:2; John 8:12)

With the room dark, ask: "Why is it dark in here?" Brainstorm how our lives would be different if we never had light. What were the first words of the Creator in Genesis 1:3?

Read Isaiah 9:2. How was the world "dark" when Jesus came? (There was no way to remove sin.)

What does Jesus claim to be in John 8:12? What must we do to have His light?

Read or sing "O Come, O Come, Emmanuel." Thank Jesus for being our spiritual light. Ask Him to remind you of this truth anytime you see a light source.

Day 3—Jesus is a purifying fire (Malachi 3:1–2; Matthew 3:11)

What are some uses for fire? (Cooking, heating, refining.)

How is Jesus like a fire? (He can remove the impurities from us.) Read 1 Corinthians 3:7–15. What three building materials can be burned? What three can't?

What does it mean to build with gold, silver, and precious stones? (Do things that please the Lord.) During a time of candlelight meditation, reflect on personal thoughts and actions of the day and ask forgiveness for those not pleasing to Jesus.

Day 4—Jesus is the True Vine (Isaiah 11:1–2; John 15:1)

How are evergreens different from trees with leaves? (They have needles and keep their color year-round.) If possible, look out the window, and contrast an evergreen with a bare deciduous tree.

What is Jesus called in Isaiah 11:1–2? (God's branch.) Why will the greens on our wreath eventually die? (They have been cut from the main trunk.) According to John 15:5, how can Christians be like uncut evergreens? (Abide like branches in Jesus, who is the vine, or trunk.)

Read John 15:9–14. How does Jesus say we can "abide" in Him? (Obey His commands and love one another.) Read or sing "Away in a Manger."

Thank Jesus for His love; tell Him how much you love Him. Ask Him to use evergreens to remind you of your relationship to Him.

Day 5—Jesus is Priest and King (Psalm 110:4; Hebrews 5:5–6)

Identify the colors in the Advent wreath. Why do the candles differ?

What color was the robe mockingly placed on Jesus (John 19:2)? Purple was worn by priests (Exodus 25:4; 28:4–5) and kings (Daniel 5:19). What person in the Old Testament was both a priest and king (Genesis 14:18)? What person in the New Testament was (Hebrews 4:14; Revelation 19:16)?

What does Jesus do for us as our High Priest? (Intercedes to His Father for us; provides a perfect sacrifice of our sins.)

What does Jesus do for us as our King? (Rules over our lives in righteousness.)

Praise Jesus for His sacrifice and sovereignty.

Day 6—Jesus is God in flesh (Psalm 2:7; Romans 1:3–4)

Here is a trick question: Does God have a body? (Compare John 4:24 with John 1:1, 14.) God is a Spirit, but in Jesus He has a human body.

Why is one candle the color of our skin? David (remember the giant he defeated?) foretold Christ's birth a thousand years before it happened. Read Psalm 2:7 and Romans 1:3–4. The skin-colored candle represents Christ living in flesh.

What other kind of body does Jesus have (Ephesians 1:22–23; Colossians 1:27)?

Thank Jesus for being God and man. Thank Him for coming to live in your body (or ask Him to if you haven't). Ask Him to remind you as you look in a mirror that He lives in you. Read or sing "One Day."

Day 7—Christ is seen in His people (Isaiah 42:6; Matthew 5:14–16)

Read Isaiah 42:6. Who other than Jesus is the light of the world (Matthew 5:14–16)? What are we forbidden to do with our light? What are we to do with it?

Discuss how your family could reach out with Christ's love. Think of ways your Christmas decorations, greetings, and celebration could bear more distinctive light for Jesus. Ask God for His wisdom and creativity in making His Son known to others.

Read or sing "Joy to the World!"

Read any Christmas cards that have arrived since the last session and pray for the senders.

Hundreds of years before Jesus was born, His "birth certificate" was accurately completed. During the next two weeks, create a birth certificate for Christ, patterned after one of your own.

Day 8—Christ would be a male (Isaiah 9:6; Galatians 4:4)

What clues do Genesis 3:15 and Isaiah 9:6–7 provide for determining whether the Savior would be male or female?

What titles does Isaiah give Jesus in 9:6–7? What activities does he predict?

How are Adam and Jesus alike (Romans 5:12–21)? How are they different?

Thank Jesus for becoming a man to head a new "race" of all who will receive His righteousness.

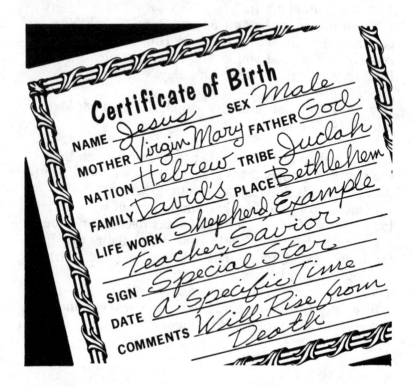

Make a creative birth announcement for Jesus, using Isaiah 7:14 and 9:6–7. Or make a poster-sized birth certificate to hang during the holidays.

Day 9—Christ would be born of a virgin (Isaiah 7:14; Matthew 1:23)

Assign character parts for the reading of Luke 1:26–38.

Count the number of times virgin appears in this passage. What does it mean? Why was it important that Jesus be born of a virgin? (To fulfill Isaiah's prophecy; so He could be holy, untainted by sin.)

Read or sing "Silent Night! Holy Night!"

What special confirming sign did the Lord give Mary (Luke 1:36)? Who was the special son born to Elizabeth and Zacharias (Luke 1:57, 63)?

Memorize Luke 1:37. Thank God for the miracle of Jesus' virgin birth and other Bible miracles. Praise Him for miracles He's performed for you.

Pretend to be newspaper reporters interviewing John the Baptist. Use Luke 3:1–20 as background for questions and responses. Tape record the results.

Day 10—His name would be Jesus (Isaiah 53:6, 12; Matthew 1:21)

Look up the name Jesus in a Bible dictionary. (It means "Savior.") What's the Old Testament equivalent? (Joshua.)

Without disclosing what you are reading, read Isaiah 53 from a modern version. Ask who the passage is about and when it was probably written. (Isaiah penned these words about Jesus more than seven hundred years before His birth.)

From this passage, what do we learn about how Jesus saves His people from their sins? (He gave Himself as a perfect sacrifice.)

Read or sing "That Beautiful Name."

According to Romans 6:23, what penalty must be paid for sin? What is God's wonderful gift mentioned in the same verse? How can we obtain it? (Read or recite John 3:16.) Praise God for the gift of His Son, forgiveness of sins, and everlasting life.

Discuss what kinds of gifts would help us remember the selfless sacrifice of Jesus. Think about the "gift of ourselves" that might be given to other family members through coupons good for a car wash, floor wax, lawn trim, or even a hug.

Discuss what gifts Jesus would like to receive from us, such as promises to read the Bible, memorize Scripture, pray, or help others.

Day 11—Christ's nation would be Hebrew (Genesis 18:18; Matthew 1:1)

Look at Matthew 1:1–16. If you were writing a book, would you begin it like this? Why does God do so? (This is Jesus' family tree.)

How far back does Matthew follow Jesus' genealogy? (To Abraham, the first Hebrew.) How far back does Luke go? (Adam.)

Read Matthew 1:1–16, and stop at names you recognize. Share what you know about him or her. Consult a Bible dictionary. Conversationally thank God by name for these people.

How far back can you trace your family tree? From memory, draw out as much as you can. Then compare notes. Contact your oldest living relatives or consult a family Bible record to extend your genealogy. Thank God for those in your family tree.

Day 12—Christ's tribe would be Judah (Genesis 49:10; Matthew 1:2–3, 16)

Genesis 49:10 compares Christ to what animal? Consult an encyclopedia for characteristics of lions that might parallel Jesus' traits. What is the lion's relationship to other animals? (King of the beasts.)

Read John 19:19 and Revelation 19:16. How must we respond to the King of kings (Philippians 2:10–11)?

Read or sing "Come, Thou Long Expected Jesus."

Day 13—Christ's family would be David's (2 Samuel 7:16; Matthew 1:6, 16)

Summarize from your reading of 2 Samuel 7:1–15 the story of David's desires to build God a house. David didn't receive what he desired, but God gave him a better gift.

In 2 Samuel 7:16, what did God promise him? Why could only Christ fulfill this? (Jesus is the only everlasting descendant of David; Hebrews 13:8.)

After reading 2 Samuel 7:18–29—David's prayer response to God's gift—and James 1:17–18, write a prayer to express your gratitude for all God's good gifts. Wrap your prayers as a gift for Jesus to be opened and read again on His birthday.

Day 14—Christ's mother would be Mary (Isaiah 7:14; Luke 1:30–31; Matthew 1:24–25)

Pretend you are detectives looking for clues about Mary's character and spiritual life. Search in Luke 1:26–56 and Matthew 1:18–25. Work as pairs or teams if young children are involved.

Share findings, then discuss evidence against Mary's sinlessness. (She acknowledged her need of a Savior in Luke 1:46–47; see also Romans 3:23.) How did God help Joseph accept Mary's condition?

Read or sing "There's a Song in the Air." Thank God for Mary and Joseph.

Mary believed God could do the impossible. What are you trusting Him to do today?

Week Three / More Prewritten History About Christ

The Old Testament presents more than three hundred prophecies in both words and symbols about Jesus' first coming. This week consider seven more that can be added to Christ's birth certificate.

115

Day 15—Christ's Father would be God (Psalm 2:7; Matthew 1:20, 23)

Read Jesus' prayer in John 17, and note how many times and ways Jesus acknowledged His equality with the Father.

Read Matthew 6:25–34, and thank God for everything you learn about Him as a Father.

Pray together Jesus' suggested prayer in Matthew 6:9–13. Memorize and recite Matthew 6:33.

Day 16—Christ would be born in Bethlehem (Micah 5:2; Matthew 2:1)

Joseph and Mary lived in Nazareth. How did God arrange Mary's trip to Bethlehem (Luke 2:1–7)?

Re-enact Joseph and Mary's attempt to find lodging. Let children knock at different doors in the house and receive responses of "No room." Finally, allow them to stay in the garage or basement.

The name *Bethlehem* means "house of bread." What connection can you make between this name and Jesus? (Look up *bread* in a concordance, or use these references: Matthew 4:4; 6:11; 26:26; Mark 6:39–44; John 6:1–14.)

Read or sing "O Little Town of Bethlehem."

Day 17—Jesus would be a Shepherd (Isaiah 40:10–11; John 10:11, 14)

Read Psalm 23 and thank the Lord for benefits we receive when He is our Shepherd.

Compare Jesus' shepherd role in these passages: John 10:11, 14; 1 Peter 5:4; and Hebrews 13:20. What will He do for us in each role?

Read or sing "While Shepherds Watched Their Flocks."

Day 18—A special star would mark His birth (Numbers 24:17; Matthew 2:1–2, 9–10)

Who made the stars? (Compare Genesis 1:16 with John 1:1–3.) There are an estimated 10 octillion stars in the universe. Write 10 followed by 27 zeroes. What does this tell us about God's power? Can you recall miracles that show Jesus' power over nature?

Thank Jesus for His great love and power. Ask Him to remind you of His creative power every time you see a star, even artificial Christmas stars.

Read or sing "As with Gladness, Men of Old."

Day 19—Christ would come at a specified time (Genesis 49:10; Daniel 9:27; Galatians 4:4)

Use a New Testament survey book or other background book to summarize ways God prepared the world for Christ's coming.

What preparations does Matthew 24–25 say will precede Jesus' second coming?

Share how God specially prepared you to receive Him; then thank Him for it. Ask Him to prepare people for whom you have a spiritual burden.

Advanced Bible students would enjoy Robert Anderson's unrefuted classic, *Coming Prince*, which mathematically and historically explains the prophecies about the time of Jesus' first coming.

Day 20—Christ would be a Savior (Isaiah 53:6; Luke 2:11)

Use these passages in Isaiah to summarize the gospel: 1:18; 64:6; 53:1–12; 44:22; 45:22.

Practice sharing the gospel with each other.

Make a felt or paper banner with graphics and these words: "Jesus came to pay a debt He did not owe because we owed a debt we could not pay."

Day 21—Christ would rise from the dead (Psalm 16:10; Jonah 1:17; 1 Corinthians 15:3–4)

Dramatically tell the story of Jonah. What does his experience illustrate about Jesus (Matthew 12:39–41)?

Form two teams to read 1 Corinthians 15:1–22. Have one team look for the consequences if Jesus were *not* alive, the other for the proofs that He *is* alive and the consequences of His resurrection.

Read or sing "Hark, the Herald Angels Sing."

Create homemade symbols for some of the previous prophecies to decorate your Christmas tree or to use on packages. Or ask children and teens to draw scenes from the Christmas story, in order, on a long piece of shelf paper.

Week Four / Why Jesus Came the First Time

The word *incarnation* literally means "God in flesh." God became a man in Jesus without ceasing to be God. Explore some of the reasons He came in such a way.

Day 22—Jesus came to reveal God (John 1:14, 18)

Without the Bible, how much would we know about God? About Jesus? What words or thoughts come to mind at the mention of God? Of Jesus?

Assign parts for an impromptu role play of the dialogue in John 14:1–14. Ask children or teens to draw their conception of God.

Read or sing "Thou Didst Leave Thy Throne." In conversational prayer, worship God for who He is and what He has done.

Day 23—Jesus came as our example (1 Peter 2:21)

Read or sing "Footprints of Jesus."

What is the example Jesus gives us in 1 Peter 2:20–24?

What sufferings did Jesus endure other than crucifixion? Can you recall any time when you suffered for doing good?

If we more often asked, "What would Jesus do?" what difference would it make in our lives?

Day 24—Jesus came to be a Savior (Luke 2:11)

In preparation, wrap three gift boxes for Jesus (something gold, perhaps a block of metal sprayed gold; a fragrant, sweet spice, such as clove; and a nonsweet spice, such as basil or dill).

On Christmas Eve, after lighting the purple candles, light the flesh-colored one. Turn off the room lights, and softly sing "Silent Night! Holy Night!"

Ask the eldest to read the Christmas story from Luke 2:1–20 and Matthew 2:1–12.

Have the children open the presents for Jesus as you explain the gifts of the wise men. The gold may have financed the flight to Egypt (it is equated with money for a journey in Matthew 10:9). The spices may have been stored and used to anoint Jesus' body. The non-sweet spices symbolized death and burial (John 19:38–40).

Stand around the Advent wreath and hold hands. Thank Jesus for coming to be our Savior.

Day 25—Christmas Day

On Christmas Day add a large white candle (for Christ's divine nature) to the center of the wreath.

If you have young children, have a birthday party for Jesus. The cake may be in the shape of a star or manger. Sing Christmas carols or hymns about Christ's birth. Present gifts to Jesus, including the one He wants in Romans 12:1–2 (see Day 10 also).

Have a worship time around the Christmas tree (if you have one). Invest the tree with extra meaning by considering ways trees or wood were associated with Jesus' days on earth (manger He was laid in, boats He rode in, cross He was nailed to, and so on). For young children, ask more direct questions, such as: "What material was used to make the manger in which the baby Jesus was laid?"

Later when the tree is taken outside, as a family cut off all the branches except two that would form a rough cross. Strip off the rest of the needles, and store the tree for Easter, when it can again be brought inside in its stand and draped with a dark cloth on Good Friday and a white cloth on Easter Sunday morning. (A smaller version could be made from a slice of the trunk with a branch nailed horizontally.)

Extend your family's learning for this month by writing prophetic Scripture on cards and placing them in a bowl for members to draw out and read at mealtimes.

Other Books by Terry Hall

Bible Panorama (Victor)
Dynamic Bible Teaching with Overhead Transparencies (Cook)
*Getting More from Your Bible** (Victor)
How to Be the Best Sunday School Teacher You Can Be (Moody)
*New Testament Express** (Sonpower)
*Off the Shelf and Into Yourself** (Victor)
*Old Testament Express** (Sonpower)

*Leader's guide for group study is available by the same author.

Popular day-long seminars based on material in this book are available. Audience involvement, colorful visuals, and creative learning methods are incorporated. For more information on how your church or organization can sponsor a seminar on creative teaching or personal and family spiritual growth, contact the author at Media Ministries, 516 East Wakeman, Wheaton, IL 60187 (312/665-4594).

Moody Press, a ministry of the Moody Bible Institute, is designed for education, evangelization, and edification. If we may assist you in knowing more about Christ and the Christian life, please write us without obligation: Moody Press, c/o MLM, Chicago, Illinois 60610.